Methodist Theology

"Doing Theology" introduces the major Christian traditions and their way of theological reflection. The volumes focus on the origins of a particular theological tradition, its foundations, key concepts, eminent thinkers and historical development. The series is aimed at readers who want to learn more about their own theological heritage and identity: theology undergraduates, students in ministerial training and church study groups.

Titles in the series:

Reformed Theology – R. Michael Allen
Lutheran Theology – Steven D. Paulson
Anglican Theology – Mark Chapman
Baptist Theology – Stephen Holmes
Catholic Theology – Matthew Levering

Methodist Theology

Kenneth Wilson

t & t clark

Published by T&T Clark International
A Continuum Imprint
The Tower Building, 11 York Road, London SE1 7NX
80 Maiden Lane, Suite 704, New York, NY 10038

www.continuumbooks.com

British Library Cataloguing-in-Publication Data
A catalogue record for this book is available from the British Library.

ISBN: 978-0-567-03427-4 (hardback)
　　　978-0-567-64498-5 (paperback)

Typeset by Newgen Imaging Systems Pvt Ltd, Chennai, India
Printed and bound in Great Britain

Contents

Preface

My intention is to invite the reader to engage with the creative conversation of the Methodist tradition of theological enquiry. Indeed, I suggest, Methodism is remarkable for its determination to explore the liberty into which it believes humankind has been delivered through Christ, and the consequent openness to and excitement about the world of God's creation. Engagement with the way Methodists have talked with God and about God over the last three hundred years cannot but open up the whole world of theological enquiry. What does it mean to believe the gospel, to accept God's grace and to affirm God's presence in Christ?

Methodist theology, when it is true to its founder, John Wesley, begins in thankfulness, and is confirmed in the desire to embrace God, to explore God's creation, to enter into the gamut of human experience in history and to share in the world of human imagination. Thus in attending to Methodist theology we must take account of all the ways in which theological enquiry within the catholic tradition engages with the many other disciplines of human experience and attempted to make sense of them.

I shall suggest that Methodism's openness to enquiry means it is well-placed to contribute to the renewal of Christian belief. It is currently fashionable in the West to dismiss theology and indeed religious faith. Some fundamentalist expressions of the Faith collude with this either by privatizing faith and refusing to engage with the world, or trying to control the world on the basis of faith. We know that neither approach is possible. Truth is alive and must be publicly explored: control of the world is out of the question. It is my contention that the lively curiosity of Methodist theology, its willingness to learn from all manner of sources and to engage with the world so as to transform it, provides a stimulus to vital reflection on the wholeness of human experience.

The Methodist theologian, when true to the tradition, does not withdraw from the world but fearlessly engages with it.

It is hard to see what the alternative could be. The three centuries since the foundation of Methodism have seen the most enormous changes in the public and personal worlds of human experience. Consider: we have known political convulsions, world wars, globalization, economic transformations, environmental pressures, population growth, urbanization, revolutionary scientific discoveries with their subsequent technical applications, the Enlightenment, new approaches to the human psyche and the nature of consciousness.

Methodism shares in the anxiety and excitement of discovery but keeps to the fore the fundamental questions which we ask one another. Why is there something rather than nothing? What is it to be a human person? Who is Jesus whom we call the Christ? What sense have we of ourselves as free persons? What do we stand for and what can we hope for? These are the questions which focus Methodist theological enquiry. In living with them, Methodism is alive to insights and initiatives whether from the theologian, the philosopher, the scientist, the economist, the sociologist, the poet, the novelist, the philosopher or the artist. All is grist to our mill and has implications, for example, for our contribution to moral enquiry. How could it be otherwise, given our confidence that this is God's world, in which God lives to fulfil God's purposes?

There is, it is said, no doctrine specific to Methodism which marks its unique stance; certainly there is no doctrine which separates us from the one, holy, catholic and apostolic Church of the creeds. It is not doctrine which led the spiritual movement of Methodism to become an independent ecclesial body. However, the more one looks into the influences which inform Methodist theology, and the openness with which it has explored them the more one is impressed by its catholicity, tolerance, inclusiveness, breadth of vision and the range of its concerns. Perhaps this is the hallmark of its individuality. It is intent on holding together the natural human curiosity to understand our faith, with an open confidence in God's gracious presence. In order to do so it assumes that theological enquiry is shaped by scripture, tradition, reason and experience.

It is my view that one will not understand Methodism unless one recognizes that it is Catholic, Orthodox, Anglican, Protestant and non-conformist, and that it has in principle always been so. It is eclectic in its approach to theological enquiry, taking nourishment anywhere it can. Our founder, John Wesley rediscovered God, or rather believed himself to have been found by God. He took that experience seriously, fed on the scriptures, read widely in the Church Fathers and drew on traditions which are identifiably Catholic and Orthodox. He was profoundly influenced by pietism, especially the Moravians but also by the Jesuits. Yet he remained an ordained priest of the Church of England to the end of his days, building on and reflecting on his experience of this Established and once powerful denomination. He accepted the truth embodied in past experience, yet abhorred nostalgia: the future would be better than the past. He had no protectionist mentality; he looked for growth and development towards a new creation fashioned perfectly by God.

Charles Wesley imprinted a lively, confident hope in God's presence on the consciousness of Methodists as they sang the hymns he wrote for them. Their catholicity has led to their prominent inclusion in the hymn books of many Christian traditions.

It is the combination of curiosity, acceptance of tradition, openness and inclusivity that informs the important role, far beyond its size, that Methodists have played in the Ecumenical Movement in which it has been involved from the very beginning. Latterly too, Methodism has been at the forefront of Christian conversation with the other major faiths of Hinduism, Buddhism, Judaism, Islam. We want to know and are keen to find out where and in what ways people of faith can work together in the service of 'God' and in the interests of human flourishing.

Methodist theology is far from being a private 'thought-experiment'; Methodists have followed John Wesley's example in wanting to and actually trying to change the world. The Methodist Church is a missionary movement directed towards the well-being of all humanity in every respect. Loving God means loving God's creation and all God's people, including the poor, for their own sake. Where is the Spirit of God at work in the world? With what suffering of the Risen Christ are we called to identify ourselves now?

Methodist theology is not dogmatic: Methodism knows in whom it believes and is focused upon bearing witness to God that the world might see and believe. Methodist theology is open, enquiring and attentive to God and the world. It is a theology grounded in God's free grace, full of hope. It is a theology of 'joy in the presence of the Crucified'.[1]

Kenneth Wilson
West Bradley Advent 2010

Chapter 1

Foundations

Methodist Origins

Methodism currently numbers about seventy-five million people in some one hundred and thirty countries.[1] But when did it begin? It is not easy to say, though there is historical evidence which dates the rise of Methodism with some accuracy. Is not the conventional view correct? Methodism, as we know it, came into existence in England in the eighteenth century through the inspired preaching of John Wesley, an ordained Anglican priest. This is of course true; but it is misleading to regard John Wesley's Methodism as a new feature of Christian history.

In order to understand where Methodism stands in the history of Christianity we have to look at a bigger picture. The British scholar Rupert Davies, rightly in my opinion, argues that movements analogous to Methodism have emerged from time to time throughout Christian history. They arise from personal experience of the reality of God's presence, the assumption of a disciplined spirituality and the urgent desire to bring the gospel to the unchurched and the poor. If this meant suffering for their calling, so be it. From the very beginning if these movements came into conflict with the Church, it was rarely on doctrinal grounds *per se* but through personal or institutional conflict. They were determined at all costs to preach the gospel in the face of political or ecclesiastical opposition.

Davies draws attention for example to Tertullian and the Montanists in the second and third centuries, Valdes (later known as Peter Waldo) and the Waldensians[2] in the twelfth and following centuries and the Hussites at the end of the fourteenth and beginning of the fifteenth centuries.[3] The latter in particular were precursors of the Reformation, Jan Hus (1372–1415) was influenced by the writings of the Englishman John Wycliffe, when they spread across Bohemia after the marriage of Anne of Bohemia and Richard II of England. Methodism is not an idio-syncratic eighteenth-century development within Christianity which sprang fully formed from John Wesley's head; it stands in what may be called a non-conformist tradition.

It is important to affirm right at the beginning that Methodist theology is not sectarian. Methodism did not seek to be an eccle-sial body, but rather to be a style of spiritual life within an existing body, the Established Church of England. It stands firmly in *the* catholic tradition of Christianity. Methodism is well aware that serious human conversation with God and about God did not begin with the birth of Methodism or indeed with the person of Jesus Christ: it is as old as humanity. Neither is it any part of Methodism's self-understanding, therefore, that illuminating Christian conversation about God and with God is now confined to Methodism. On the contrary, it enjoys the fact that the Christian Faith has from the time of Christ and the Early Church drawn on earlier traditions, and itself spawned many directions of theological enquiry; this is clear from even a cursory reading of the New Testament and slight familiarity with the history of the Early Church.[4]

Methodist theology joins the conversation which God has ini-tiated with humankind and responds to Jesus' call to take up the Cross and follow him. In accepting this awesome responsibility, Methodist theologians have wanted to learn from and build rela-tionships with other Christian traditions, Catholic, Orthodox, Anglican and Protestant: they continue to do so. Moreover, they acknowledge that insight about God and God's lively activity may be found in other religious traditions, Hinduism, Buddhism, Juda-ism, Islam and Sikhism. This is how it comes about that Methodism has made, as we shall see, a disproportionate contribution to the Ecumenical Movement and to Inter-Faith Dialogue.

II

European Theological Context

It is now generally accepted among scholars that Methodism in England was one of the most successful expressions of a widespread

Evangelical awakening across Europe which quickly extended to North America.[5] It emerged during a period of wide-ranging religious controversy involving internal upheavals within the Roman Catholic Church and conflicts between the theologians of the Reformation.

The Great Schism (1378–1417) marked the nadir of Papal fortunes during which popes and anti-popes competed for power; it was resolved in 1417 when the Council of Constance (1414–1418) elected Martin V. The Council also resolved that in order to prevent the scandal of future schism no pope should be elected without the consent of a Council. But the papacy worked hard and successfully to reconfirm papal primacy during the fifteenth century by centralizing power in Rome. This coincided with the Renaissance and its influence on the Church's erudition, aesthetic and cultural distinction but there was no comparable appreciation on the part of the Papacy of its spiritual responsibility. Papal corruption flourished through the sale of offices and rampant nepotism which spread to all levels of the Church.

But the age was remarkably religious. For example in Germany where the Church was at the heart of society and priestly authority enormous, religious life was marked by worship of the Saints, the cult of Mary, the power of relics, the celebration of masses to limit purgatory for oneself and/or for the dead, the use of the rosary and a great increase in the practice of confession. The Papacy exploited this religiosity to raise money for its secular purposes by the sale of indulgences and demands for ever greater taxes which were naturally resented and exploded in the coincidence of a desire within the Church for reform and the objection of political authorities to collecting taxes for Rome.

The Protestant Reformation began in Germany and Switzerland and was carried through northern Europe by the conversation of travellers and the power of the printing press. The critical culture of the Renaissance provided the intellectual ground for serious theological questioning. Erasmus (1466/9–1536), the great humanist scholar, set a pattern for what might almost be called 'free-thinking'.

He never himself directly challenged the authority of Rome, because he side-stepped ecclesiastical authority by directly addressing the growing number of educated laity. He was widely read in classical literature; he mocked pilgrimages, bogus relics, the trivia of religious debate and the worldliness of secular and religious clergy. He produced carefully edited versions of Western Fathers, Irenaeus, Cyprian, Ambrose and Augustine and translations into Latin of Eastern Fathers who had hitherto been unknown or neglected including Origen, Athanasius and John Chrysostom.

A striking achievement was the new edition of the Greek New Testament which he produced in 1516: it was based upon the best available sources with a new parallel Latin translation which identified certain difficulties with the Vulgate. This initiative of Erasmus focused attention on the Bible and offered new ways of approaching its meaning which essentially brought into question the authority of the Church as the sole arbiter of interpretation. Translation of the Bible into the vernacular would have a profound impact. Tyndale's English translation appeared in 1526 and Luther's German translation of the New Testament in 1522.

The sixteenth and seventeenth centuries in Europe saw challenges to the Papacy and the emergence of divisions in the Church with which we still contend today. What authority does the papal office have? What respect is due to bishops, priests and monks? What role does the laity have?

Luther, Zwingli, Melanchthon and Calvin, the major theologians of the Reformation, challenged the Papacy in their commentaries on scripture though they did not all sing from the same hymn sheet as became apparent from 1529 onwards: they differed on matters ranging from sacramental theology to the relation of ecclesiastical to political authority. With what authority did the Church exercise power and over whom? What authority was rightly possessed by the Prince? The Lutheran tradition divided the Empire which led to recognition by the Imperial Diet of Augsburg (1555) that the religion of each state should be that of the ruler, Lutheran or Roman Catholic.

Erasmus crossed swords with Luther regarding the latter's belief in predestination when he affirmed the essential significance of human freewill. Was personal salvation predetermined by divine will or was faith open to all, subject only to the willingness of the individual to accept, by grace, God's free offer of forgiveness?

4

These and related questions emerging from the Reformation were not resolved by debate between the contending theologies.

The rise of Protestantism strengthened the forces of reform in Roman Catholicism. The Council of Trent (1545–1563) was called by Pope Paul III to deal with disunity and indiscipline within the Church. It was intended to bring about reconciliation with Protestantism since the ecclesial structures were not yet irrevocably divided. In the event, however, its decisions pushed the Catholic Church and Protestantism further apart. Council decrees, for example, affirmed the Vulgate as the biblical text, and declared the Church the sole interpreter of scripture. It confirmed the seven sacraments, the doctrine of transubstantiation and repudiated Lutheran, Calvinist and Zwinglian doctrines of the Eucharist. The canons following the decree on Justification declared the Protestant doctrine of Justification by Faith to be anathema. Celibacy was required of all priests and seminaries established for priestly formation. The Council did however renew discipline and reinvigorate the Church's spiritual life. St Francis de Sales (1562–1622) and St Charles Borromeo (1538–1584) exerted a major influence on the laity's practice of the faith by encouraging prayer and spiritual reading.[6] The ubiquitous presence of the religious orders, especially the Jesuits, provided nourishment, teaching, spiritual vigour and example.

The implications for the future of the Church stemming from the competition between Lutheranism and Calvinism together with the spiritual revival of Catholicism continued unresolved through the conflicts political, ecclesiastical, religious and spiritual of the seventeenth into the eighteenth century. The persecutions, cruelty, civil wars, movements of population, personal conflicts and theological misunderstandings hidden within the awful events of the Thirty Years War (1618–1648) remained even after the Treaty of Westphalia in 1648 had in principle recognized the religious pluralism of Germany.

In this den of theological argument, and political revolution there arose an Evangelical Awakening. It consisted of movements, societies, associations of Christians within the Church, both Protestant and Catholic, focused on setting a spiritual example to the wider Church. The movements within Protestantism, however, saw themselves as missionary enterprises that were inclined to question the decisions of both political and ecclesiastical authorities when they appeared to be in conflict with the authority of Christ, and what they took to be the plain meaning of scripture. Above all, any interference with the freedom to preach the gospel was intolerable.

The religious societies within Protestantism fulfilled a function not unlike that of the religious orders in Roman Catholicism because, like them they were free to roam. Both Protestant societies and Catholic religious understood the importance of attending to local culture if they were to commend Christ among backsliders and unbelievers. The societies of the Evangelical Awakening rarely conflicted with ecclesiastical authority since they took care to remain publicly orthodox in belief and practice. When they did get into trouble it was usually because their success and growing influence temporarily fell foul of the local bishops jealous for their own power and authority.

Many societies and groups flourished in this maelstrom of passion. Personal piety was an important feature of them all. The Moravian Brethren deserve special mention because of the impression they made on John and Charles Wesley. They traced their origin to the Hussites, Protestants before Protestantism, in the early fifteenth century. In 1722 Count Nikolaus von Zinzendorf (1700–1760) had welcomed to his estate at Herrnhut a party of Austrian refugees driven into exile by the advancing Counter-Reformation. He identified himself with their quiet pietistism which was personal, Bible-based and dependent upon each individual accepting for himself God's forgiveness. Encouraged by Zinzendorf, the Moravians became a dynamic missionary force. The members were lay and therefore free to travel unencumbered by loyalties other than to Christ. They were, notwithstanding early association with the Lutheran Church, independent of ecclesiastical discipline. Moreover, they kept themselves as free from conflict as they could by focusing on the task of bringing the gospel to places without a formal Christian presence. Missionaries went, for example, from Herrnhut to work in the West Indies (1732), North America (1735), South Africa (1736) and Labrador (1752).

John Wesley's England

John Wesley was fully aware of these forces and influences, theological, personal and political. Turmoil and dramatic change were apparent in the English Church and State, too. The recent history of England had included Civil War in the seventeenth century when a challenge to Divine Right and the royal prerogative had resulted in disruption of local communities and produced conflicting loyalties within a family. The war had formally ended with the Restoration of the Monarchy in 1660, but many questions remained from the republican period concerning the nature of authority. At the same time, union with Scotland in 1707 brought about a new sensitivity to and pride in Englishness as also did the beginnings of imperial expansion. A new cultural freedom characterized the confidence of England in its political and military power, its civilization and growing wealth. Theatres, concert halls, books and journals including *The Spectator* gained influence while entrepreneurial deals and louche conversation flourished in the coffee houses.

Associated with this was a worldly excess which earned the condemnation of preachers and religious writers alike. William Law (1686–1761), a profoundly spiritual man, wrote in 1726 against the theatre and in support of Christian Perfection. His most important work *A Serious Call to a Devout and Holy Life* published in 1728 had greatly influenced John Wesley when he read it in 1729, as it did later the Tractarian, John Keble. In all his writings Law commended an uncompromising Christian life focused on the love of God and the service of others.[7]

Amidst all this confusion, the Established Church struggled to maintain unity and to hold society together. It faced changes in public understanding of the world and challenging new philosophies: it was divided in its attitude to the state, concerned about the condition of society and corrupted by wealth and indiscipline. But despite these disturbing aspects of Anglican life, the ecclesiastical corruption often adduced as the primary reason for the rise of Methodism can easily be exaggerated. Some bishops did condone the indolence of prosperous parish clergy who relaxed in the fleshpots of London and retained poorly paid and often uneducated, if nevertheless sincere, curates in their parishes to look after the cure of souls. But there were good bishops, faithful parsons and intelligent curates. Indeed the fact that Methodist societies were often encouraged by serious-minded parsons and flourished to start with alongside other religious societies within parishes suggests that piety and the desire for a holy life were far from dead in the Church.[8]

Thomas Bray (1656–1730), for example, rector of Sheldon in the English Midlands responded to an appeal of Henry Compton, bishop of London, to go to Maryland to support the Church. In anticipation he established the Society for the Promoting of the Christian Gospel (SPCK) in 1698 to meet the educational poverty of the clergy in the colony and set about establishing libraries; he departed for Maryland the following year. Experience swiftly convinced him that an English base would better meet his educational ambitions. He returned home, focused the SPCK on education and founded the Society for the Propagation of the Gospel (SPG) for mission. Bray saw the essential need for oversight if the Church in New England was to flourish as Wesley did later when in Georgia: neither succeeded in persuading the respective bishops of London to act.

While there are clearly similarities between the SPCK, the SPG and Methodist societies there is a fundamental difference. The SPCK remains an independent society, but is nevertheless closely linked with the Church of England: the SPG is a Church society, authorized by Convocation and incorporated by Royal Charter. Their control remained in principle with clergy, a feature which distinguished their ecclesiological position from that of the Moravians and, as we shall see, the Methodists.

The time would come when John Wesley could no longer pretend that he had done no more than begin a spiritual movement within the Established Church. When he and the early Methodist preachers were banned from preaching in parish churches by bishops, John Wesley revolted against their heavy authority. In his opinion their attitude prevented the poor hearing the good news of salvation through Christ.

Enlightenment, Non-Jurors and Latitudinarianism, Population Growth

Three particular features of life in the nation and the Church should be mentioned for their impact on Wesley and the way in which Methodist theology developed in dialogue with them: empiricism, the divisive influence of the non-Jurors and population growth.

First, the empirical philosophy of Bishop George Berkeley, John Locke and David Hume emphasized the pre-eminence of reason and the 'scientific method'. It was influential though this does not imply that English society was becoming more secular since religious belief remained significant in both personal and public life.

Wesley was not opposed to Enlightenment thinking, nor was Evangelicalism in general or Methodism in particular a response to secularization.[9] Actually, John Wesley was intrigued by the insights into God's creation opened up by empirical enquiry and built on them insofar as he understood them. He took things at their face value, and included as 'facts' reports of wonders that we would now dismiss. Thus, for example, cures mentioned in his *Primitive Physick,* were 'what worked'.

He was unsurprised that one could learn of God through studying his creation and perhaps apprehend the supernatural. His faith was not challenged by empiricism for he thought that while human enquiry could describe the marvels of the physical world he, no more than John Henry Newman, believed that a scientific account of human experience could be given which excluded the religious and the spiritual.[10] And as for reason, while we may suspect the conclusions to which Wesley is led by his use of his reason, that he believed reason relevant to discussion of faith and belief is beyond question.

Secondly, the Enlightenment did not so much lead to the rise of secularism as challenge the Faith and remind the Church of the need for perceptive theological enquiry. Latitudinarianism associated with the Cambridge Platonists, Benjamin Whichcote (1609–1683), Provost of King's College, and Ralph Cudworth (1617–1688), Master of Christ's College was influential in stimulating theological reflection.

The Cambridge Platonists were committed to conformity within the Church of England, and in the face of political conflict and theological dispute were more concerned with comprehension and tolerance than adherence to a strict doctrinal position, ecclesiastical order or liturgical practice. Hence in the face of the new empiricist philosophy, the remembered political conflicts of the seventeenth century and the threat to the coherence of the Church of England their affirmation of a reasonable faith informed eighteenth-century sensibilities.

They feared religious bigotry and focused on the business of holding things together in Church and State. Arminian in theology they affirmed that humankind was endowed with divinely given free will which would liberate humanity from prejudice and injustice. Reason, personal insight and the indwelling of God's spirit in the human mind meant that it was possible to discern the will of God, be faithful to Christ, live wisely and grow in understanding. They grasped after a *Summum Bonum* which they believed they would identify given time and which everyone would share.

Wesley was familiar with their significant influence in the Church of England: some of their themes resonate with Wesley's thinking. Reason, the indwelling of the Spirit, the desire for order and the expectation that perfection was not beyond human grasp, through God's grace were all important to Wesley.

Their approach to argument was consistent with the eighteenth-century notion of politeness.

> Politeness created a complete system of manners and conduct based on the arts of conversation. . . . Traditional Christian works saw life as a journey, a passage from this world to the next, observed by God; politeness represented the world as a theatre in which one was obliged to perform before one's fellow men.[11]

Politeness was how a gentleman would express himself in society; reasonable conversation would bring different opinions into a dynamic unity to the benefit of society. This cultural assumption may be an influence on the Methodist practice of 'working together in conference' in order to achieve unity.[12]

The Church of England was provoked in 1688 by the refusal of some clergy, Bishop Ken (1637–1711) of Bath and Wells, and eight other bishops among them, to take the oath of allegiance to William and Mary on the grounds that it would break previous oaths sworn to James II. William Law was removed from his fellowship of Emmanuel College, Cambridge when he refused to take the oath. The use of Act of Parliament to debar them and appoint successors was unthinkable to the non-jurors, for whom it undermined the basis of ecclesiastical authority. By whose authority was it that persons were preferred to office in the Church? Was it by the authority of God and Christ in his Church, by the King or by the King in parliament? They were clear that the answer was God and Christ through the courts of the duly Established Church. Their position was reminiscent of the seventeenth-century Caroline divines whose theology made a major contribution to the later formulation of a distinctive Anglican churchmanship; High Church, catholic and reasonable. The issue remained live throughout the eighteenth century. Ecclesiastical authority concerned John Wesley both with regard to Methodism within Anglicanism and later within Methodism.

Thirdly, growth in the population and the migration of people from the country to the towns were significant in national life. However, industrialization is now reckoned to have taken place more slowly than hitherto assumed. Moreover, such population growth as took place, was a feature of both rural and urban life. Growth in town population was local, mostly in the south and south west and in some northern cities, such as Sheffield, Newcastle and Leeds. Urbanization as we know it is a feature of the late nineteenth century.

These features reveal an England excited by growing knowledge of the physical world, intrigued by the questions it stimulated for sensitive and practical theological enquiry and concern about population growth.

V

The Beginning of the Methodist Movement: Methodist Societies

The Methodist movement had fertile ground in which to grow – England was a society passionate for the gospel. The ambivalence of the Established Church to authority, its concern for unity, its manner of thinking through its theology in response to the Enlightenment and the weakness of its influence through corruption and indifference meant that the Church was often unconnected with society. The consequence was that there were many abandoned, dispossessed and poor, who were unchurched. Furthermore the country had an expanding population, the beginning of imperial expansion and a growing economy – all of which threatened the status quo and made many fearful of disunity.

It was association with Moravians that focused Wesley's attention on God and stimulated a new awareness of the liberty into which he had been born in Christ. John and Charles Wesley met a group of Moravians in 1735 when they voyaged to America to support the Anglicans in Georgia: they were mightily impressed by their steadfastness in the storms on the voyage, by their discipline and their earnest devotion. They remained in touch with them in Georgia. When they returned to England in 1738 after their dispiriting missionary enterprise they sought to renew their faith and hope by meeting with Moravians, in particular with Peter Böhler. John Wesley and Peter Böhler established a Moravian Society in a church in Fetter Lane. Wesley records it in a journal entry for 1 May 1738. It proved to be a crucial decision for the brothers Wesley and for Methodism.

The Methodist Movement is rooted in the personal experience of John Wesley, when God came alive for him on 24 May 1738 at a meeting of the Fetter Lane Society in Aldersgate as he listened to Luther's preface to the Epistle to the Romans. Later in the year John Wesley went to Germany to talk with the Moravians at Herrnhut. The visit was not entirely successful, as it provoked misgivings in Wesley's mind regarding their 'quietism' and reliance on justification by faith alone. On his return to London matters came to a head in the Fetter Lane Society. On the one hand, the Moravians could not cope with Wesley's assertion that faith meant also good works. On the other hand, Wesley's Arminianism implied that since the entire world could enter into the liberty of God's children, quietism was tantamount to indolence. He could not stay quiet, left the society and launched his own United Society. Thus it was that Methodism emerged in the context of the Anglican Church through contact with the pietistic faith of Moravians.

There are many interpretations of 'the heart strangely warmed' of the 24 May 1738. Was it a real conversion or did it confirm a faith which he already possessed? Was it the occasion when he understood what it really meant to accept the free gift of God's forgiving presence? Suffice it to say that Wesley's life was transformed so that he set about the task of bringing the world to Christ with whole-hearted enthusiasm. Since then the conversation which is informed by and which flows from that experience has been taken up in the several Methodist traditions. Methodism is not shy of talking about God: experience counts!

There is no special revelation behind the emergence of Methodism; it makes no claim to be new. Its genius was and is, as a society within the Church (originally Anglicanism but now more widely within the universal church), to respond to, think through and embody the power of God in Christ in preaching the gospel and living out the Christian life. For those unfamiliar with Methodism this can in fact be one of the most confusing things about it. Baptists are committed to adult baptism, Catholics to the magisterium and the authority of the Pope. Is there a *Methodist* theology? What does Methodism have to say about God that is not said in other religious traditions? Nothing. Where then does Methodism stand? Is it possible to identify and develop one distinctive, coherent Methodist theological position?

But is this the point? Methodism stands within the orthodox tradition of Christian faith and develops theology on the hoof. On the one hand, the task of stating 'Methodist theology' is rendered more difficult by the divergent experience of Methodist societies as they took life in their respective localities. Even the assumption that there is one coherent theology in the British Isles is unhelpful since Welsh Methodism, for example, differs substantially from English Methodism. In Wales the influence of Rowland Harris (converted in 1735) and Lady Huntingdon was Calvinism as opposed to Wesley's strong Arminianism. Most particularly in England, Methodism was shaped by the theology of Anglicanism within which it came into existence as a society. In North America where there was no Established Church, Methodist theology responded flexibly to the very different social circumstances.

Moreover, it is not merely the social environment which has influenced Methodist talk about God. Methodist ministers, lay

13

persons and theologians think through for themselves the intellectual and moral challenges presented by the results of intellectual enquiry, of science and technology, economics, philosophy and aesthetics. This undoubtedly makes putting together 'a Methodist theology' more complicated but all the more interesting. Nevertheless I believe it can be done.

VI

Some Principles of Methodist Theology

Methodism inherits through Wesley the riches of Christian theology as found in the Catholic, Orthodox and Protestant traditions. Methodist theology holds together doctrine, public worship, personal piety and good works and regards them to be in principle indivisible. I outline briefly some principles of Methodist theology from which it draws strength.

First, it is focused on God, knowledge of whom is a gift of God's grace: it is not the product of unaided human effort. But the gift has to be unwrapped, and this is no simple matter. It involves hard work, a lifetime of it for the individual believer and a period as long as human history for humankind.

Secondly, we know that we have entered into the marvelous Christian tradition of reflection about God and strive to find our place in it so that we can contribute to the conversation out of our own experience. Methodist theology is therefore attentive to the whole gamut of human reflection on God in its many inter-related forms, theological, philosophical, moral, aesthetic, historical, mystical, empirical and metaphysical. Following Wesley, we want to engage everyone in conversation – the believing, the perplexed, the doubting, the cynical and the unbelieving. Indeed, it is part of our humanity to recognize that from time to time we are all perplexed, doubting, cynical and even unbelieving. With Terence the Roman dramatist we can say, there is nothing human which is foreign to us.[13] Nothing human is foreign to God; nothing human can be foreign to us. Methodists are grabbed and excited by what we are capable of learning about our world in all its diverse and contrasting relationships: we want to make sense of it all in the light of our faith in God as revealed in Christ.

Thirdly, Methodists believe that theology is a form of enquiry: the truth about God and God's relationship with the world has to be sought, it is not just given. Thinking about God is an activity as is all worthwhile thinking – there is no such thing as passive thinking: doctrine is not 'received'; it is worked for and worked at. Moreover as Wesley perceived, properly understood, thinking is transformative of the self not a matter of collecting facts or being imprinted with information.

Fourthly, this feature of thinking draws attention to the fact that to enquire is more than an intellectual exercise narrowly defined; it demands as any genuine education does, a commitment of one's whole self. It was Simone Weil who pointed out that to give attention to something, to an idea or to another person is a voluntary activity which involves the whole person in the effort to give oneself in relationship to the other.[14] There is necessarily an aesthetic, moral, spiritual sensitivity to the wholeness of things which has to be respected if one is to learn something and know that one has learned it. Attending to Christ, giving attention to the Bible and the Christian tradition shares these features: they bring us to ourselves.

Fifthly, the theology which emerges from creative enquiry has to be tested in experience. This is done not only in one's personal life but openly in community. Methodism tests practical policies intended for the betterment of the whole of society 'in conference'. In this manner, we recognize that God-talk will only be understood, affirmed and its dynamic nature identified as it is debated in public, expressed in practice and subsequently questioned in the light of experience.

Sixthly, Methodist theologizing is a continuing process so Methodism, when it is true to itself, cannot be authoritarian. It does not declare a divinely received truth and require every member of the Church – let alone the world in general – to accept and believe it without question. Indeed what comes to be recognized as valuable in the tradition, and in the process of enquiring as one engages with it, is the result of careful attention to what one believes one is learning combined with a continuing will to re-evaluate it in the light of experience. It must never be forgotten that other potentially conflicting claims to truth will arise that need to be brought into the conversation. Methodism is not utopian. Utopian idealism rejects any need for further intelligent enquiry because one is convinced that what one believes is identical with revealed truth, vouchsafed to oneself but denied to others. A utopian believes he has a duty to impose his convictions on others. This is exactly the contrary of the Methodist position which holds that truth has constantly to be explored with others. Methodist theology is authoritative, not authoritarian: its authority arises because in the light of experience, the Methodist finds that God, revealed by Christ, the Bible, the creeds and the tradition are worthy of trust.

So, seventhly, for Methodists theological enquiry is not a private matter; it involves conversation, not simply with contemporaries, but with the generations of enquirers whose work has been discussed, published and thought about for centuries. Hence scholarship and wisdom are appreciated and sought.

Eighthly, this dimension of theologizing is embodied within the Methodist tradition because of the emphasis on 'conference' – the meeting together with others with an open enquiring mind to determine, if one can, what *at present* is believed to be God's will. This is why authority lies (especially in British Methodism) in 'Conference'. But even here, the actual authority depends upon the willingness of all Methodists to recognize it which in turn hangs upon the quality of the debate, its discernment and charity. Conference decisions carry weight because they are continually subject to review and debate: Authority is never handed over completely to any external body because properly understood Conference is not an 'external body'. Conference has authority because each Methodist is in principle a part of it and able to contribute to the debate whenever it seems appropriate. The point about engaging in 'conference' is that Christ and his truth are alive and not finally understood.

Conference may potentially be authoritative, never authoritarian – as I have said above but it bears repetition: Methodism does not believe in utopias: there is always the possibility of error, failure to discern the truth and moral turpitude. Sin is rampant in all human affairs. – including Methodism.

Ninthly, Methodism gathers up all it understands, feels and believes into the thanksgiving of Eucharistic worship, where we celebrate the fact of God's presence with God's people in creation. We receive Christ's body and blood in the bread and the wine and go out into the world 'in peace in the power of the Spirit to live and work to God's praise and glory'.[15]

VII

Conclusion

So what does this add up to for Methodist theology? We hold an orthodox vision of God as he reveals himself in Christ. We believe that God is continuously making our world through the living presence of his gracious spirit, affirmed and expressed in the life, teaching, sacrificial death, resurrection and ascension of Jesus Christ and in the work of his Church.

Could we sum it up in this way? Wesley knew where he stood, but looked for new understanding, deeper devotion and a way of talking about the faith which would move people to accept God's forgiving love for themselves. I think we should think of Wesley's approach to theological enquiry as closely analogous to that of Professor Kenneth Grayston, a distinguished English Methodist New Testament scholar who established the department of theology in the University of Bristol, England, and was the first Chair. He called his inaugural lecture, '*Theology as Exploration*'.[16] In my view, that is how Wesley thought of theology and how Methodists have thought of it since. We have, of course, to consider the notion of exploration in a broad sense. For Wesley exploration implied a personal risk which arose from taking the gospel out into the unknown world of faithlessness and despair, in order to spread scriptural holiness across the land.

This was a huge ambition: from the very start, Wesley's mission was not confined to England but included Wales and the state of Georgia in North America. He was inspired by a sense of the universal presence of God which he thought of as the free grace of God given in creation and in the life, death, resurrection and ascension of Jesus Christ. God was present in everything and in everyone – in principle. Wesley was called to bring awareness of God to life in every person. This was the theology which inspired him and made sense of his vision. Following Paul's deepest insight, he accepted that nothing in heaven or earth could

separate us from the love of God in Christ Jesus our Lord.[17]

Hence opposition, doubt, conflict, confusion, intellectual puzzle-ment, moral disquietude – all imply the importance of exploration.

Wesley is often referred to as a dictator, ruling his society with a rod of iron. It is true that he believed God required that a faith-ful disciple be true to his word and accept discipline. He felt that a responsibility had been laid upon him to exercise it over others when occasion required. But he acknowledged that he may have mistaken the way himself as he states in the preface to his *Sermons on Several Occasions.*

> But some may say I have mistaken the way myself,
> although I take it upon me to teach it to others. It is
> probable many will think this; and it is very possible that
> I have. But I trust, whereinsoever I have mistaken, my
> mind is open to conviction. I sincerely desire to be better
> informed. I say to God and man, 'What I know not, teach
> thou me!'[18]

This style of thinking, inseparable from action, has inspired Meth-odist thinking about God from Wesley's time until our own. As Wesley took the road on horseback to preach, he also took the road metaphorically as he read and wrote in order to keep the gospel engaged, relevant, intelligent, believable and redemptive.

John Wesley, the founder of Methodism in its contemporary form, was not an academic theologian who retained roots in the university but he was a scholar. It was as a priest and scholar that he became so powerfully convinced of the importance of accept-ing God's invitation to converse with him, that he could not refuse the vocation to invite others to join him.

Chapter 2

Preaching and Singing the Faith

I

Introduction

The England into which John Wesley rode was anxious. Both Church and State were concerned to maintain stability after the religious and political conflict in previous centuries. They shared an ambition to build a sense of nationhood, to take advantage of incipient imperial power and to exploit scientific developments which offered potential benefits especially in agriculture and industry. Religious belief, however, flourished; societies emerged within and outside the Established Church to support the spiritual aspirations of those who sought God. Many, however, never heard the gospel preached because the Established Church was remote, sometimes indifferent and wary of enthusiasm.

Wesley had accepted objectively that he was a Christian when an undergraduate in Oxford; he had tested his calling in Georgia and returned despondent. But the experience of 24 May 1738 awakened a passionate concern to proclaim the gospel. Fired by God's love for him Wesley wanted to engage the world in conversation with God so that all could enjoy the freedom which flowed from accepting God's forgiveness. It dawned on him that while salvation was freely available for all through God's grace, they could only respond if the gospel was brought to them. So he launched himself on a lifetime of preaching. With remarkable speed the Methodist Movement became the most successful English expression of the European Evangelical revival that emerged from the religious conflicts of the sixteenth and seventeenth centuries.

II

Commending the Gospel

Sermons were for Wesley more than means to an end – bringing people to faith: he was concerned for the way of truth. Thus, although Wesley may have left no tomes of systematic theology, he explored theological themes in his preaching in order to involve his 'congregations' in conversation with God. God and God's love for all creation are at the heart of all that he says. His understanding of God, however, means that there is work for man to do. God is omnipotent and committed to perfecting the world which he is creating. However, consistent with his nature of love he cannot 'force' faith: even such language is nonsensical. Hence there is a critical role for the preacher. His task is to point to the loving presence of God and to commend faith in Christ who reveals the Father and gives himself for the salvation of the world. What this means Wesley works out on the hoof.

He begins in scripture. Wesley is moved by the story of God's loving-kindness for the people of Israel as revealed in the Old Testament. God does not remove them from the face of the earth or abandon them when they are disobedient; he is ever-present and courteously attentive to the well-being of his people, as he had promised in the covenant he had made with Abraham. And when Wesley turns to the New Testament, he is overwhelmed by what he intuits of God, not just about God, in Jesus Christ. God not only cared about his world in a detached manner, he had personally committed *himself* to it and was working for its salvation. Jesus Christ in his life, teaching, sacrificial death, resurrection and ascension reveals God to be absolutely consistent in his love of humankind and of all creation. Nothing could bring God to abjure his nature of self-giving love: nothing could deprive humankind of the potential flowing from the knowledge and love of God.

St Paul's vision of God was underpinned by this life-giving insight. Whether in storm at sea, addressing the faithlessness of churches, alone with his fears, or in prison – whatever his circumstances, St Paul was convinced that nothing could separate him from the love of God in Christ Jesus. Indeed, he was certain that this was true for all humanity since God would deny his own nature if he did not intend to complete what he had begun. John Wesley shared St. Paul's confidence. He yearned, like St Paul, to save souls but knew that no power on earth could compel faith. Preaching was the way, he believed, to call the people's attention to God's good news and offer God's grace which they had the God-given freedom to accept or reject it.

Jesus stood in the line of the prophets as the model for the scholar-preacher. He addressed people where they were in their own language. He reminded them of God's loving presence to forgive by involving them in the stories he told which drew on their experience. Wesley embraced Jesus' example which had been followed earlier by the orders of friars established by St Francis and St. Dominic. Indeed, the Dominicans to this day glory in their official title *Ordo Praedicatorum* – The Order of Preachers, OP. Methodism in this regard as in others stands four-square in the main tradition of the Evangelical Faith – both Catholic and Protestant. Methodism is a preaching and teaching order.

Wesley's generous sympathy for ordinary people was stimulated by Jesus' compassion. He did not patronize them but dignified their status by striving to include them in lively conversation with the Word of God in scripture, and in principle with the Fathers, with the catholic tradition and with the Reformers. He preached salvation for all, rich and poor, through faith in Jesus Christ. He wanted them to worship in the parish church but his passion for souls led him to challenge Episcopal authority when, as it appeared to him, its exercise prevented the free flow of God's grace. As an Anglican priest, he did not take kindly to the thought of open-air preaching, but he felt compelled to do it when denied access to parish pulpits. His behaviour (and even more that of some of his itinerant preachers) on occasion provoked public unrest, even violence. He was accused of enthusiasm which implied not only horrid irrationalism in a culture of polite reason, but threatened social cohesion. Yet, his words gave voice to the voiceless and spoke to the heart. Indeed, many Anglicans, clergy and laity believed he spoke God's truth and found their faith renewed.

John Wesley believed that anyone who is alive in Christ is free, free from sin; but he knew it was a disciplined liberty. Salvation does not free a person to do or believe whatever he fancies and still call himself Christian, let alone Methodist. To live a Christian life means responsible, spiritually aware, intellectually and personally creative theological enquiry; but there are limits. This was clear to John Wesley as he set out to preach the gospel and to Charles Wesley who composed the hymns in which Methodists sang the Faith. Methodism has no Roman Magisterium, but it knows there must be discipline in doctrine and in life. Moreover, converts needed the support of others if they were to grow in the faith so in the absence of firm parochial structures, Wesley brought local groups of converts together in class meetings, eventually linking them together in a system of pastoral oversight across the Connexion.

III

The Sources of Wesley's Preaching

On what did Wesley base his authority? In principle the answer is God in whose presence he had absolute confidence. His focus was on the Trinitarian God, Father, Son and Holy Spirit; he was his inspiration and vision. What are the sources which he employed in his preaching? John's sermons and Charles' hymns drew on the four classical dimensions of the Faith – the Bible, tradition, reason and experience.[1] The intention was to engage the world in conversation with God and engage the faithful in the business of working out their own salvation.

i) Scripture

Scripture is the common source for all Christians of the knowledge and love of God. John Wesley believed it to be the inspired Word of God. Born as he was at the very beginning of critical work on the Bible he was unconcerned about the authorship or the date of books of the Bible. What concerned him was the meaning in the search for which the diligent, faithful reader would be guided by the Holy Spirit. Above all scripture was a source of nourishment, spiritual, intellectual and moral for all Christians. Certainly John Wesley thought of it in this way: the scriptures were the primary source of all true thinking about the nature of God and God's relationship with the world. Most particularly he believed this because the God who is celebrated in scripture is revealed to be the Creator of the world and all that therein is. Moreover, the Bible declared God to be a loving God who loves what he has made and is determined to bring it to perfection by committing himself to its well-being. As a living guarantee of that commitment he gives himself to the world in Jesus Christ. This is the God the Bible reveals; he is the God in whom Wesley believed, whom he loved, whose presence he celebrated and in whom he trusted.

If one is to know God for oneself, the implication was, one must learn to read the Bible for oneself. We know that reading is an empowering activity which engages the whole person; certainly that is so when one reads the Bible. Wesley urged disciples to take the Scriptures seriously and 'read, mark, learn and inwardly digest them'. Wesley takes to the text all that he is, his circumstances, knowledge, experience, what he felt, what he believed and what he admired. As he worked to 'make sense' of the Word he was at one and the same time learning about God and making sense of himself. The truths of the Bible are to be imbibed and made a part of who one is so that what one believes and what one does will be consistent with one's sincere desire to grow into the pattern of the life of Christ.

But the Bible has to be interpreted to be believable: texts cannot be swallowed like pills. Wesley recognized that apart from attention to the Bible as a whole, individual books, let alone individual texts, may be misleading and misinterpreted, which will frustrate the possibility of a genuine Christian life. Hence the sermons draw on multiple references and quotations in any effort to explain the meaning. To assist his preachers Wesley published *Notes on the New Testament* in 1755 in which he commented on the Authorized Version in the light of Bengel's Greek text of 1734, and *Notes on the Old Testament* in 1765/1766.

To read the Bible or to hear the Bible read, is to enter a demanding world of puzzlement, enquiry and praise which, Wesley believes, reveals the depth of the love which God offers to the world. God's love is not rationed, it is unmerited and free.

Actually God cannot ration his love, because God's love is God. And neither can one earn it by 'doing what one is told'; there is no *quid pro quo*. In one sense, of course, we must be obedient to the Word of God because we are called to continue in our own lives God's conversation with his creation. But to do this requires 'intelligent' obedience which involves working at the meaning and testing it in experience. To refuse to exercise our God-given freedom is sinful, because in doing so we fall short of the glory of God and take no account of the fact of God's living presence. So we are back where we started! To listen to the Spirit and to make progress in faith requires personally demanding hard work. And so it should if, as Wesley suggested, biblically based theological enquiry is to be transformative of the self and potentially of the Church and of society.[2]

Wesley's experience confirmed it. The disillusionment he found in his own 'far country' Georgia, brought him like the prodigal son to himself and to God. At a meeting of a religious society in Fetter Lane already referred to above, he found himself lifted out of his directionless life and made whole as he listened to Luther's commentary on Romans. The experience was personal – he knew that God loved the world but now he experienced God's love for him and discerned the spiritual reality beyond, within and behind the text. In his language he might have said that he was given a sense of the presence of God with him and of being at one with God in Christ, notwithstanding his sense of unworthiness. He tried to work out what this meant in the rest of his life, in preaching, teaching, evangelizing, in prayer and worship and in his many writings.

Wesley learned to read the words of scripture as an introduction to the story of God's salvation of the world and was liberated by it. God's freedom was open to all as the experience of the Chosen People testifies and Jesus promises. To involve the world in this life-giving story was Wesley's purpose. But the crowds whom Wesley addressed were largely illiterate and uninvolved in worship so he chose the oral medium of preaching. All his preaching began with scripture, the Word of God.

John Wesley's sermons and Charles Wesley's hymns are inspired by and take their authority from the Word of God. Wesley's intention was to deliver its message, after due research and prayer, in ways that his hearers would find consistent with tradition, reasonable and intelligible.

ii) The Creeds of the Church

A second source of Wesley's preaching and of Charles' hymns is the creeds, the product of the Church's struggle over many centuries to agree words which say what they believed about God, Father, Son and Holy Spirit. The many-faceted vitality of Methodist theology is grounded in the fullness of the Christian tradition, including the creeds. John Wesley was familiar with them from his upbringing in an Anglican rectory and his time at Oxford University as undergraduate and Fellow of Lincoln College. The creeds focus on God, Creator, Redeemer and Sustainer. They affirm the incarnation, crucifixion, resurrection and ascension of Jesus Christ who triumphs over sin, offers forgiveness and eternal life to all. They were regularly on the lips of believers through their use in the worship of the Church.

As a student of the Fathers, Wesley was familiar with their ways of thinking: he was an orthodox believer. But to understand what orthodoxy amounts to is no simple matter. For some it implies adherence to a fixed revelation, but not for Wesley nor for Methodist theology.[3] Suffice it to say at this point, that as already indicated above, for Wesley and for the subsequent Methodist tradition, theological enquiry is a lively personal (as opposed to an individualistic) activity; it is more than an attempt to remember and restate things which have been said before. It looks for continuities; it seeks to grasp insights and explore them so as to test whether and how they illuminate the tradition; it is anxious to take into the process of theological reflection everything that is found valuable from every area of human enquiry and to incorporate it in faithful living. There is more than a little in common here with Newman's approach to doctrine.

> The more claim an idea has to be considered living, the more various will be its aspects; and the more social and more political is its nature, the more complicated and subtle will be its issues, and the longer and more eventful will be its course.[4]

iii) Reason

The liveliness of doctrine must have been familiar to Wesley given the wide range of his reading. But he held to what Newman was later to call the preservation of type, the continuity of principles and the unitive power of faithful developments. Thus, for theological enquiry to be significant, coherent, intelligent and believable it has, thirdly, to be reasonable, as the Cambridge Platonists also affirmed. We have seen that Wesley's thinking about the faith took place in the context of the Enlightenment. The thinkers whose ideas were current in the eighteenth century were hostile to all unconsidered authority in matters intellectual. Locke, Berkeley, Hume and Kant, for example, in their various ways presumed the priority of reason, observation and experiment. 'Scientific knowledge' provided essential information which should be taken into account in any reflection on our human condition. It provided insight into 'the nature of things' and could not be ignored if one sought for truth.

Wesley was inclined to a similar view since it embodied a dynamic attempt to describe the material world of God's creating, and offered opportunities for enhancing human well-being. It did not lead him to believe, however, that confining truth to what the philosophers in the light of empirical enquiry called 'rational' covered all that could be truly apprehended given the experience of the human. The worlds of the imagination and the aesthetic were integral with the 'rational', and indeed essential to it. Wesley would have warmed to the contemporary view that the results of scientific enquiry involve the imagination in the design of experiments and the interpretation of the evidence. Mathematicians are well aware that simplicity and elegance are two important features of truth in mathematical enquiry.

iv) Experience

To limit the pursuit of truth to the rational would have eliminated the fourth basis of his preaching, personal experience. Human beings had an awareness of a world which included the empirical and the rational but which was beyond the merely rational when they tried to give a true and full account of themselves and of their world. To be rational in this sense does not include all that is implied when one talks of what it is to be reasonable.

On the contrary, the power to observe, to organize experience for experimental purposes and to think clearly, may be consistent with the claim that human beings function well when they think rationally, but to be reasonable implies common sense, an acceptance of the emotional and the aesthetic, a capacity to stand in awe and wonder. It is an important consideration in establishing, maintaining and developing relationships with other persons, with the world of which we are a part. It is also a dimension of our relationship with God. Reasonableness takes account of the fact that human beings are persons who must learn to think with the whole of themselves and learn like God what it is to give one's whole attention to others. The doctrine of the incarnation embodies this truth.

It is therefore of profound significance that in the Christian tradition God is referred to as 'personal', or as Tillich said, 'the ground of our being'. Wesley, and Methodists ever since, have claimed that we discover our humanity through recognizing what it is for God to be thought of as 'personal being', and trying to live out the personal relationship with God which is revealed in Jesus Christ, embodied in scripture and explored in tradition. God is not 'a' person but the ground in which all personal being finds its substance. Wesley's conversion was the occasion when he met God personally and discovered the person he (Wesley) was.

The Church looked for a distinctive statement of God's nature. After more than three centuries of thought, prayer and controversy, it settled on God as Trinity, Three-Personed God. Paradoxical as it may appear, this is how the Church identifies and points to the dynamic unity of God, Creator, Redeemer and Holy Spirit. Though often underemphasized or even ignored, it is the paramount doctrine in Wesleyan and subsequent Methodist theology.

IV

Proclamation

The basic theological themes alluded to above underpin the sermons of John Wesley and the hymns of Charles. Their preaching and singing brought Methodist societies into existence and encouraged their maturity. So what in fact did John preach, and Charles sing? They constituted the contemporary media through which those who flocked to hear them were introduced to the gospel and learned their theology. Proclamation, teaching and celebration were three dimensions of the one Faith, as far as John Wesley was concerned. Their importance for a society on the move is that they were oral: sermons lent themselves to discussion and debate; hymn singing built a sense of belonging in a community of faith.

In expounding and developing a Methodist theology it is vital to recognize that since it is grounded in scripture it is dynamic and practical in character. There is nothing static, fixed or domesticated about the way in which Methodism has gone about its theologizing. The Bible is free and open for all to read. The Living God calls for a personal response through lively thinking, intelligent conversation, obedience to the law, prayer and regular worship: only thus will the Spirit inspire faith and encourage it. Learning how to read the Bible, how to give it attention is of the first importance.

Wesley understood his calling to be the spread of scriptural holiness throughout the land and, as it transpired, throughout the world. Speaking the Word was the means available to him since many of those whom he saw to be in need of salvation were illiterate. But what did Wesley mean by preaching and what did he hope to achieve by it? He thought of it from the two perspectives of gospel and law. In a letter to 'My dear friend', dated 20 December 1751, Wesley writes:

I mean by 'preaching the gospel' preaching the love of God to sinners, preaching the life, death, resurrection and intercession of Christ with all the blessings which in consequence thereof are freely given to true believers.

By 'preaching the law' I mean explaining and enforcing the commands of Christ briefly comprised in the Sermon on the Mount.

I think the right method of preaching is this. At our first beginning to preach at any place – after a general declaration of the love of God to sinners and his willingness that they should be saved – to preach the law in the strongest, the closest, the most searching manner possible, only intermixing the gospel here and there and showing it, as it were, afar off.

After more and more persons are convinced of sin, we may mix more and more of the gospel in order to 'beget faith,' to raise into spiritual life those whom the law hath slain; but this is not to be done too hastily either.

His first words were to remind his hearers of God's loving presence and only then to draw attention to the liberty of their forgiveness. Given the common view that Wesley sought to provoke instant conversion, his remark here that raising into spiritual life is not to be done too hastily is worth noting. Of course some may 'see the light' in a flash of inspiration, but the hard work of learning what it means and trying to put it into practice takes time.

Wesley explains his approach to writing sermons in the preface to his published sermons: it is very instructive.

I sit down alone: only God is here. In his presence I open, I read his book; for this end, to find the way to heaven.
Is there a doubt concerning the meaning of what I read?
Does anything appear dark or intricate? I lift up my heart to the Father of lights: 'Lord, is it not thy Word, "If any man lack wisdom, let him ask of God"? Thou "givest liberally and upbraidest not". Thou hast said, "If any be willing to do thy will, he shall know". I am willing to do, let me know, thy will'. I then search after and consider parallel passages of Scripture 'comparing spiritual things with spiritual'. I meditate thereon, with all the attention and earnestness of which my mind is capable. If any doubt still remains, I consult those who are experienced in the things of God, and then the writings whereby, being dead, they yet speak. And what I thus learn, that I teach.[5]

Here in a nutshell is the pattern of Methodist thinking about God and God's gracious concern to bring the world to perfection and all persons to salvation. First, recall that you are in the presence of

God; secondly, attend to the words of scripture; thirdly, recognize the difficulties and see whether they can be resolved by looking at other relevant passages of scripture; fourthly, enter into conversation with experts in the field, remembering that this conversation must include those who have died, but who have recorded their thoughts in published works.

This is reminiscent of what Michael Oakeshott claimed to be the true purpose of education – to equip a student to enter into the conversation between the generations.[6] Above all it is a conversation which never ends; as far as Wesley was concerned this was certainly so, because the beginning and end of the conversation is God. Exploration, *par excellence*!

Wesley preached to convict the hearer of sin and bring him to himself. His intention was to provoke the hearer to accept God's proffered forgiveness and stimulate a lifelong growth in faith. No doubt the printed sermons were edited for publication: nevertheless reading them today convinces one of the seriousness with which Wesley gave himself to the business of bringing the Faith to the people and the people to faith. Forty-four of them continue to provide standards of preaching and belief by which the witness of the Church to the Christian experience of salvation is secured.[7] They cover every dimension of Christian life and doctrine and outline the liberty of faith in Christ as Wesley experienced it. He affirms God's presence, calls for repentance and offers forgiveness. He offers practical advice on the use of money, warns against bigotry, commends a catholic spirit and takes up many themes from the Sermon on the Mount. Wesley introduced people to God and to scripture and urged them to take up the conversation for themselves.

V

Taking the Gospel to the World

Though John Wesley was and remained an ordained clergyman of the Church of England, he believed that he could not but follow the example set by Jesus: if the people will not come to him he must go to them. He was not the first as we have seen; St Francis, and St Dominic and many others followed the same road. The opportunity arose through George Whitfield whom he had met in Oxford and who had followed Wesley to Georgia. Whitefield had begun in 1739 to preach in the fields to the rough colliers of Kings Wood in Bristol and found them astonishingly responsive; thrilled by his success he wrote inviting John Wesley to join his Bristol missionary enterprise. After careful reflection and much prayer he accepted and took to the fields of Kings Wood.

This was a move with which his brother Charles profoundly disagreed. So did the bishop of Bristol, Bishop Butler. Wesley claimed that as an ordained priest of the Church of England and a Fellow of an Oxford College he had freedom to preach any-where; a view not shared by the good bishop. But he was inspired by the people to whom he preached. In fact, it was as early as 11 June 1739 that Wesley wrote in his Journal, 'I look upon the world as my parish'. John Wesley was not to be deflected from his mission by what he felt to be the mistaken exercise of Episcopal power.

Indeed he launched by example waves of itinerant preachers with his encouragement and authority who spread out across the world to preach the gospel, call men and women to accept God's forgiveness and pursue the possibility of Christian perfection. This occurred first in England, then in other parts of the British Isles, and across the territories of the emerging British Empire, such as the West Indies. Their enthusiasm was also mirrored in North America with the passionate example of Francis Asbury who was ordained as General Assistant in America by Thomas Coke in 1784 from which date the effective independence of the American Methodist Church can be dated. Itinerant preachers, unrestrained by Episcopal authority, accompanied the trek west-ward across the States proclaiming with confidence the gospel's message of hope. Their success was prodigious.

Wesley was true to his word: the world was his parish. Method-ism has inherited this vision and throughout the nineteenth and twentieth centuries right up to the present day has continued to be a missionary society.[8] The impact on Methodist theology has been wide ranging as Methodists have engaged in conversation with the culture of each community. The conversation involved members and hangers-on at every level; the itinerant preachers, class leaders, women visitors and the laity in general were also engaged. This is a very important feature of Methodist thinking about God.

VI

Singing the Faith

Preaching was not the only way in which John Wesley involved the people in conversation with God. Preaching and the singing of hymns were of equal importance. They shaped the Methodist message and have come to be associated with Methodism itself. Methodists preach and sing their faith and their theology: the hymns became tutors in theology to congregations as they sang the words, prayed and meditated upon them. They illustrate clearly the interaction of the brothers with the world. On the one hand the preacher engaged the world in conversation with Christ with a view to bringing the hearer into a relationship with God. On the other hand the body of believers celebrated in song its sense of being a thankful community belonging to God. The former was essentially a public oral proclamation: the latter a communal expression of faith. In these two ways Methodism expressed in active form Wesley's vision of the Church as the Body of Christ given to the world and as a faithful society united in love by God's grace.

Neither was a mere repetition of conventional truisms. There was more to Methodist worship than preaching, even though that may well have been the sharpest focus. Both John and Charles encouraged liturgical prayer and Eucharistic celebration which at first he believed should be as members of the worshipping community of the local parish Church. Extempore worship occurred in the class meetings which emerged to support the faith of local Methodist societies.

From the beginning wherever the gospel was preached, praise and hymn-singing was at the heart of Methodist life. The first of John Wesley's many hymn books entitled *Collection of Psalms and Hymns* was published in Charleston, South Carolina in 1737, when the Wesleys were on their ill-fated trip to Georgia.[9] It contained hymns by Isaac Watts, the Congregationalist and others as well as by Charles Wesley. Other hymns books followed, most particularly, *A Collection of Hymns for the Use of the People called Methodists* in 1780. While John Wesley remained the publisher of the Methodist hymnbooks throughout his life, Charles was the dominant influence on Methodist hymnody.

Charles is reckoned to have written some 9,000 or so hymns, many among the best in the English language. *A Collection* contained 525 hymns, the vast majority by Charles. John wrote the preface which is very informative. He is not modest in his claims, and posterity has concurred with his judgement since many have found their way into hymnbooks of many churches other than the Methodist.

It is large enough to contain all the important truths of our most holy religion, whether speculative or practical; yes, to illustrate them all, and to prove them both by Scripture and reason. And this is done in a regular order. The hymns are not carelessly jumbled together, but carefully ranged under proper heads, according to the experience of real Christians.

In what other publication of the kind have you so distinct and full account of scriptural Christianity? Such a declaration of the heights and depths of religion, speculative and practical? So strong cautions against the most plausible errors, particularly those that are now so prevalent? And so clear direction for making our calling and election sure, for perfecting in holiness in the fear of God?[10]

In the conclusion of this paragraph of the preface he refers to the whole work as in effect a little body of experimental and practical divinity.[11] In so doing I believe he sums up his approach to theology: Wesley's thinking about God is nothing if not 'experimental and practical'.

The very structure of the hymnbook makes clear that the intention is to make it of general use: it is a book for public worship, for the class meeting and for personal spiritual reading. It is anchored in Scripture with a vast range of biblical reference and allusion from both Testaments. It is made memorable by much good poetry. The sections have a shape which covers the Christian Life. The collection begins with *Exhorting, and beseeching to return to God,* underlining the universality of God's invitation to the Eucharist. We do well to recall that despite neglect of the Eucharist in the Anglican Church, the Wesleys made it central to their evangelical concern. The 1745 publication of *Hymns on the Lord's Supper*, underlines this fact.[12]

> Come, sinners, to the gospel feast;
> Let every soul be Jesu's guest;
> Ye need not one be left behind
> For God hath bidden all mankind.[13]

It continues with a section, *Describing the Goodness of God.*

> Where shall my wond'ring soul begin?
> How shall I all to heaven aspire?
> A slave redeemed from death and sin,
> A brand plucked from eternal fire,
> How shall I equal triumphs raise,
> Or sing my great Deliverer's praise?[14]

This verse alone contains four scriptural references and one to the personal experience of his brother – a brand plucked from the burning. As a child John had been rescued from death in a fire at the parental home, Epworth Rectory in Lincolnshire.

There follows a group of hymns, *For Mourners convinced of Sin.*

> Author of faith, to thee I cry,
> To thee, who wouldst not have me die,
> But know the truth and live;
> Open mine eyes to see thy face,
> Work in my heart the saving grace,
> The life eternal give.
>
> Shut up in unbelief I groan,
> And blindly serve a God unknown
> Till thou the veil remove;

The gift unspeakable impart,
And write thy name upon my heart
And manifest thy love.[15]

Eight scriptural references in these two verses!

The encouraging pattern continues, *For Believers Rejoicing.* The absolute confidence in God's love, freely given, for all is confirmed and the believer is invited to celebrate his experience with joy and thanksgiving. The very singing of the words is intended to confirm the experience.

Thy ceaseless, unexhausted love,
Unmerited and free,
Delights our evil to remove,
And help our misery.

Thou waitest to be gracious still;
Thou dost with sinners bear,
That saved we may thy goodness feel,
And all thy grace declare.

Thy goodness and thy truth to me,
To every soul abound,
A vast unfathomable sea,
Where all our thoughts are drowned.

Its streams the whole creation reach,
So plenteous is the store,
Enough for all, enough for each,
Enough for evermore!

Faithful, O lord, thy mercies are,
A rock that cannot move;
A thousand promises declare
Thy constancy of love.

Throughout the universe it reigns
Unutterably sure;
And while the truth of God remains
Thy goodness must endure.[16]

But that is not all: there's more to come: sanctification, perfection in love is of God's intention for the world.

Groaning for full Redemption

Saviour from sin, I wait to prove
That Jesus is thy healing name,
To lose, when perfected in love,
Whate'er I have, or can, or am;
I stay me on thy faithful word,
The servant shall be as his Lord.[17]

And in the society or class meeting there is deep acknowledgement of personal faith, hope and love.

For the Society, Praying

1 Christ, from whom all blessings flow,
  Perfecting the saints below,
  Hear us, who thy nature share,
  Who thy mystic body are.

2 Join us, in one spirit join,
  Let us still receive of thine;
  Still for more on thee we call,
  Thou who fillest all in all!

7 Sweetly may we all agree,
  Touched with loving sympathy;
  Kindly for each other care,
  Every member feel its share.

10 Love, like death, hath all destroyed,
  Rendered our distinctions void!
  Names, and sects, and parties fall,
  Thou, O Christ, art all in all![18]

The theology celebrated in the hymns says everything that John and Charles wanted to share about their knowledge of God in Christ. They are theological, practical, doctrinal, direct, compassionate and personal in character. Not one person is excluded from the possibility of salvation; for God's gracious goodness has sought and found even me. I can never be sufficiently aware of the cost and therefore sufficiently thankful. My progress in the spiritual life is slow; I mourn my sins and long to see face to face my God, my Great Redeemer. I know that God is real, that his truth and love which lie at the heart of creation have authority over the whole world. Full salvation is possible for all which makes it sensible if not exactly understandable, to believe that humankind and all creation may be united in Christ. God, the rock of our salvation, frees us to attend to the well-being of one another and the salvation of the world. All our words and works can be praise.

Joyful praise and celebration is informed by the seriousness of faithful searching, prayerful devotion and profound regret to make clear the openness of the worshipper to God's word. And everything is grounded in scripture: the *Collection* indexes more than 2,600 references in the 525 hymns.

The whole gamut of Christian theology is included – the Trinitarian nature of God, Creator, Redeemer, Encourager – the source of all goodness. The Incarnation of Christ, his teaching, salvific suffering, resurrection, ascension and sitting on the right hand of God as judge. The Body of Christ the Church, alive in Christ, and the servant of the world. The work of the Spirit that sustains, teaches, enables, makes whole. And personal piety which ranges over an awareness of sin to the celebration of God's eternal presence with the communion of saints including those alive now.

There is no other hymnbook so comprehensive, so sensitive, so personal or so creative. It is exploratory, affirmative, encouraging and demanding. To sing the hymns 'whole-heartedly' is to be asked questions about oneself and to have the ground affirmed in which understanding and love of God can continue to grow.

John Wesley himself took great pride in good hymn singing as is clear from his account of a Methodist congregation in 1757.

Their solemn addresses to God are not interrupted either by the formal drawl of a parish clerk, the screaming of boys who bawl out what they neither feel nor understand, or the unseasonable and unmeaning impertinence of a voluntary on the organ. When it is seasonable to sing praise to God, they do it with the spirit and the understanding

also . . . all standing before God, and praising him lustily,
and with good courage.

This is fine stuff from which we can gauge both Wesley's likes and
dislikes – organists beware! One can hardly imagine that John
Wesley, let alone Charles would relish the contemporary theology-
free pseudo-religious ditties which pass for hymns!

VII

Conclusion

The sermons that they preached and hymns that they sang suggest
that they rejected any thought that it was necessary for a person
to accept a fixed set of doctrines before he could 'believe' and be
saved from sin. First and foremost Wesley preached for salvation,
not to inform, but to transform. And Charles wrote hymns the
singing of which 'whole-heartedly' would encourage, express
and confirm faith. Of course, there was information given in the
preaching and in the hymns, but it was 'information' about God
and God's gracious offer of salvation, not doctrinal statements in
propositional form to be noted down and remembered.

The freedom which the Wesleys celebrated is moving. They
were absolutely clear that the gospel was the free gift of God's
grace. Thus while all humankind may share in sin, so all humanity
may share in salvation: none is excluded. All may flee from the
wrath to come. Hence he had no sympathy at all for a Calvinist
position which held that the saved were predetermined by God's
action. That seemed to Wesley to be immoral and totally inconsistent with the nature of God the Father revealed through Jesus
Christ. One may not earn one's faith by good works or by faithful
practice, but without them one shows no understanding of what
is involved when one says one believes. But how was the world to
learn this and grow in the knowledge of God's gracious love?
Wesley was not the only person to answer this question but his
answer was clear, 'Lord, here am I, send me!' Methodist theology
today receives the same call and encourages the same response.

Chapter 3

Grace Abounding

Introduction

Successful professionals are educated to become reflective practitioners.[1] Brilliant examination results and theoretical knowledge are all very well, but they are only the beginning. We need to put them to the test and learn from experience in order to grow in understanding and wisdom. To all intents and purposes theory without practice is valueless. An architect needs more than theoretical knowledge when she comes to design a house. She will become a good professional, when she has acquired a feel for the location, a sense of the appropriate materials and the capacity to work with other professionals and the client. Every project is a learning opportunity. Theory is honed in practice: practice is informed by reflection on theory. This is analogous to the scientific method. We learn the theory, criticize it and learn to reshape it in the light of experiment. Theological enquiry requires a similar approach.

Wesley has, misleadingly, sometimes been dismissed as a practical theologian, as if practical theology was somehow below the salt. Nothing could be further from the truth: it is to make a fundamental mistake about the nature of theology – certainly it is a mistake in respect of Methodist theology. Theology is a practical discipline which involves living exploration, intellectual enquiry and moral endeavour: all theologians are in principle, reflective practitioners.

A Practical Theologian

We might say in current parlance that Wesley involved himself in 'doing theology'. He was no academic theologian, though he had been a Fellow of Lincoln College and was widely read. He was a reflective practitioner, steeped in the tradition, who put this theology into practice. Wesley took his theology into his preaching; but he understood that preaching was more than sermons and sermons more than words; preaching is a life-activity. He knew in his bones that theology was only intelligible if it meant something in practice. So in order to express his belief that Christ had lived and died for all, he knew that he must live a life of service to the world. This style informs all Methodist theologizing from Wesley's time until today. We are practical theologians in the sense that as persons and as a church we develop our theology in the light of experience.

John Wesley is, provided it is properly understood, rightly regarded as a practical theologian. But Methodist 'practical theology' does not lack intelligent discussion of the tradition; neither does it imply instant reaction to crises or mere problem-solving. On the contrary, Methodist theological enquiry values its membership of the Church Catholic which it evinces by its participation in the traditional conversation of faith. What is true is that Methodists understand very clearly that there is no serious involvement with the Church's theological enquiry or personal salvation which does not at one and the same time express itself in courteous attention to the needs of the world.

There is integral within Methodist theology, in the light of its Trinitarian understanding of God as Creator, Redeemer and Sustainer, an implicit vision of the good life in community, an aspiration for it, recognition that it is in principle achievable, but that it requires a committed lifetime of work.[2] So if, as Wesley affirmed, God's gracious offer of forgiveness is for all, it is necessary both to work at the vision, its underlying theological perspective and at the practical implications of this conviction. Wesley, like Aquinas and Newman, focused the whole of his theological understanding on the gracious presence of God's eternal loving kindness. On the one hand it meant preaching the gospel and taking the good news to whomsoever he could in season and out. On the other, it meant taking all practical steps open to him to meet the material needs of the poor and to search out the lost. To this dimension of Methodist theologizing we now turn. What did it amount to and what was its influence on the Methodist understanding of the nature of the Church?

III

Faithful Believing Assumes Faithful Loving

Faith does not remove the need for good works: it confirms their necessity and the opportunity for them. Wesley makes this plain in two sermons on Rom. iii, 31, 'Do we then make void the law through faith? God forbid: yea, we establish the law'.[3] The point is, he says, that faith exists to promote the eternal end of love, not to encourage the belief that with faith one has no need for holiness.

> Let those who magnify faith beyond all proportion so as to swallow up all things else, and who so totally misapprehend the nature of it so as to imagine it stands in the place of love, consider farther that as love will exist after faith, so it did exist long before it.... There was, ... no place before the foundation of the world for faith, either in the general or the particular sense. But there was for love. Love existed from eternity in God, the great ocean of love. Love had a place in all the children of God, from the moment of creation. They received at once, from their gracious Creator, to exist and to love.[4]

God, the Trinity, grounds all Wesley's theology. God is love: it is manifest within the godhead and he cannot but express it in all that he does. It therefore precedes faith ontologically.

The insight began to influence Wesley when as an undergraduate at the University of Oxford he was a leading member of the Holy Club. The club's piety was not confined to prayer, bible study and spiritual reading; members also visited Oxford jail and brought food and other necessities to widows and orphans. They were mocked for the tough discipline they imposed on themselves and nicknamed 'methodists'.

The ill-fated excursion to serve the Christians in Georgia is a further example of Wesley's theological concern and charitable sensitivity. His Journal indicates that his decision to leave Oxford was partly occasioned by concern for his own soul. But this spiritual ambition, admirable in itself, does not mean that his interest in going to Georgia was selfish. He could put his theology into practice, contribute to a new society in an unspoiled land and work among Indians who had no knowledge of the Faith: the tasks would focus any concern for his own salvation on the well-being of others. It all seemed too good to be true – and turned out so to be. But the vision which took John Wesley to Georgia should not be too easily dismissed: it had considerable influence on Wesley's subsequent development as a theologian and ecclesiastical leader.

Georgia was established in 1732 as a trusteeship under the British Crown through the initiative of James Oglethorpe (1696–1785), an English general and philanthropist. Two matters led to its foundation. First, there was a concern for the ideals of religious freedom and social enterprise including trade; secondly, political anxiety over the English Protestant Carolinas which were threatened by Spanish Catholics in Florida. Oglethorpe argued that the establishment of an English settlement between Florida and the Carolinas would provide a defence against the Spanish and an opportunity to challenge the trade of France and Spain. Moreover debtors and the deserving poor could be settled there in freedom to establish themselves with every chance of prosperity. The combination of philanthropy inspired by religious faith with political and economic interests would be very hard to manage successfully in the long term. Nevertheless, for Wesley the opportunity to share in the establishment of a new Eden where religious freedom offered the prospect of re-establishing Primitive Christianity was very attractive.

In the event there were few debtors or deserving poor; most of the English immigrants were failed shopkeepers and tradesmen. Other European immigrants arrived, especially Protestants from Germany, including Moravians. The practice of religion was free for all except for Catholics but, in the absence of any Episcopal oversight – something which Wesley tried but failed to persuade the Bishop of London to establish – competition rather than co-operation was paramount. Wesley tried his utmost in this confusing environment but with little success: Oglethorpe confined Wesley's work to the settlers in Savannah and despite personal interest he had little contact with the Indians. But the vision remained with him and there were experiments from which he learned and which fed later into Methodist practice. He began, for example a small society for mutual spiritual support; he published a hymn book; he preached freely and experienced the liberty of worship practised by the Moravians from whom he also learned that faith demanded not only intellectual assent, but personal experience of God's forgiveness.

Nevertheless he returned home in 1738 believing himself to be a failure and set about the business of re-establishing his faith on firmer ground. The opportunity came through meeting with an Anglican-Moravian Society in Fetter Lane, London. The spiritual experience already alluded to pushed him to find himself as preacher, teacher, evangelist and missionary. His renewed sense of faith led him to discern and accept the forgiving presence of God and in Christ's name to bring the Father's love to all including the poor and lost. And it was some commitment! He is calculated, for example, to have preached above 40,000 sermons in his lifetime and travelled at least a quarter of a million miles on horseback. He met the poor on their own terms and experienced the shocking conditions in which many lived – he must often have suffered from fleas and lice from literally shaking their hands. He would have found this no more pleasant than the next man, but he understood that service of the poor required that he physically met them face to face not simply, as we might say, in virtual space. How else would he understand their real needs and be able to take initiatives to satisfy them? It was not sufficient to have good feelings or to put money in a charity box. So serious was he that he gave away much of his personal income to charity.

There were of course other churchmen devoutly committed to helping the poor but Wesley's society with colliers in Bristol, miners in Cornwall and other outsiders up and down the country was regarded by many as nasty, and probably dangerous. The Bishop of

London, Edmund Gibson, was deeply offended by Wesley's sympathy for the 'rabble'. It is not clear whether he thought the issue to be fundamentally political or religious. Gibson was a High Church Whig and a friend of Prime Minister Robert Walpole who relied on him for advice on Church affairs. But did he really believe that the poor were outside God's love, or was he as a member of the establishment, concerned that Wesley might disturb the fragile political equilibrium and foment disorder? The latter is quite possible given the real threat of the Jacobites in the 1740s.

Wesley himself was like Gibson High Church but Tory not Whig; he certainly had no Jacobite sympathies. When he affirmed himself to be Tory, what he meant was that he believed God, not the people to be the source of civil power. He held together his religious and political liberties in one loyalty which combined the fear of God and the honour of the King whom he regarded as the embodiment of the nation before God. This united loyalty to Church and State, as it were, meant that he was the servant of all spiritually, morally and physically. He saw no division between being a citizen of the State and a participant in the worshipping life of the Church. However, Wesley following the experience of Jesus, may have accepted that while he had no intention to divide communities, the preaching of God's Word, would be likely to challenge the *status quo* and lead some in authority to feel threatened.

For Wesley, of course, the matter was theological and could not have been clearer; faith in God had major implications for human life and the well-being of human society. God loved all, not one was excluded: all could therefore be saved and should be offered God's forgiveness which was theirs through Christ. To confess belief in such a God was at one and the same time to be committed to putting the vision into practice. Wesley preached to the poor wherever and whomsoever they were because he assumed the unity of the nation under God and the King, and believed himself to be doing nothing more than bearing witness to it publicly. He may have needed some persuading to respond to Whitefield's invitation to join him in preaching in the fields in King's Wood, Bristol, but on reflection it seemed essential if the poor were to be reached and personally engaged in the search for salvation. As an ordained priest of the Church of England and an MA of the University of Oxford he may even have thought that he had a right to preach without the authority of the diocesan bishop or the parish priest. The extent to which this was self-justification rather than serious defence in full knowledge of canon law remains doubtful.

There is a further dimension to be taken into consideration. Wesley believed that to serve the poor was to work with Christ and that by so doing he was contributing to his own sanctification. It was good for one's soul and Wesley was concerned for his own soul. But his piety was far from simplistic. It was not the case that Wesley saw service of the poor as a means of *earning* salvation. On the other hand, while good works are no substitute for faith they are a key expression of what it means to *be* faithful. Assured of the love of God, the Christian is free to respond to the feelings which well up as a result and which lead him to want to live in love and peace with all other people and with creation.

One could almost use the language of obligation here; Wesley certainly did believe it his duty to preach to and serve the poor because too few others were doing so; they did not see it as an aspect of faith in the way that he did. But to talk of being under an obligation while true would be wholly inadequate as a sum-mary of the relationship with God which faith presupposed; Wesley did not do what he did because he felt under obligation but because he wanted to. Hence there is a generosity and cour-tesy about it which arises from his awareness of the presence of God. We are all God's children: God is our Father. That is why we can pray with Jesus and all the faithful the family prayer which Jesus taught his disciples.

Our Father, who art in heaven; hallowed be thy Name; thy kingdom come; thy will be done; on earth as it is in heaven. Give us this day our daily bread. And forgive us our trespasses, as we forgive those who trespass against us. And lead us not into temptation; but deliver us from evil. For thine is the kingdom, the power, and the glory, for ever and ever. Amen.

The significance of this for Wesley and for all Methodists is that the 'Our' is inclusive of *all* people. All stand before God in need of salvation from sin; all need their daily bread. All pray to be delivered from evil. What is more, all may have salvation and their daily bread because Christians are one in the Body of Christ, the Church, and God is Our Father.

IV

Trust the Poor

Consistent with the vision which lay behind his decision to go to Georgia, Wesley may have had a starry-eyed view of the poor but without question he had a respect for them which is evident also in the preaching of Jesus. Jesus' ministry focused on the poor and despised; he treated them with dignity and sat alongside them. Wesley evinced an analogous sympathy. He did not regard them as workshy; if they were idle it was rather because the aristocracy took the wealth of the community for their own selfish purposes. A pious aristocrat would surely have recognized his duty to provide the poor with work so that they were spared the indignity of destitution. The spiritual benefits of doing so would have accrued to both wealthy and poor.

Wesley may indeed have entertained from time to time a romantic view of the poor: he thought labour had its own God-given dignity and may even have thought the poor to be the repository of civic virtues.[5] Their behaviour, in need as they were, showed great sensitivity to the needs of others and often evinced an unconscious piety which he thought admirable. No matter how destitute they were he urged them to care for those less well off than themselves and expected that they would be able to offer assistance. There were two reasons for this. He believed first that no one whom God loved could have the spark of charity extinguished. Secondly, the personal benefit to the benefactor which resulted from the doing of good to another meant that not even the poorest was deprived of the possibility of sanctification. As a consequence it was natural for him to regard spiritual revival as almost always emanating from the poor, as it had he believed in the early days of Christianity, and decadence, scepticism and a spendthrift attitude as spreading downwards from the top echelons of society. His experience tended to confirm him in this view.

The single-mindedness with which Wesley pursued his vision has given rise to the view that he was a 'driven' man with a domineering character: once he had the bit between his teeth there was no stopping him and such was his character that he required others to follow his example. There is truth in these two judgments, I suspect. But to suggest that he could not help himself would do him an injustice. He knew perfectly well what he was doing, and he did it because he believed that he had been freed by God to do what he wanted to.

The range of Wesley's initiatives flowing from his respect for the poor which were intended to bring them honour is a measure of the importance he attached to what Randy L. Maddox has called responsible grace.[6] This informed even his view of the role of the poor in public worship. Anglican worship was confined for the most part to the Prayer Book services of matins, evensong and Eucharist. The poor, even if they were involved with the parish church regarded themselves as excluded from the Eucharist because of the impossibility of associating with respectable parishioners. This was particularly true of those who moved into the towns and lost contact with their familiar village communities. In fact even in the countryside absentee clergy, a growing population and the increased wealth of the landlord farmers often brought about the same division.

Wesley's response was to recognize the place of honest untutored speech in worship, and in the spiritual life of the class meetings and bands which were established to nourish the faith of the converted. Lay persons led the class meetings which met weekly to care for the spiritual well-being of the converted. There were prayers and Bible study in which all shared, and a poor fund to which each contributed a penny a week to support the needy. Charity was not confined to members but extended more widely when need was identified. The class meeting marked the wholeness of a faithful life: it sustained the physical needs, moral well-being and spiritual growth of each member, and a concern for the whole community. As the number of Methodists grew, classes and societies were brought into association in circuits which were further linked to form the Connexion.[7] Wesley appointed local preachers and itinerants to look after them who could be drawn from any class of society.

Of course Wesley did not celebrate poverty for its own sake and admire it as if it was the proper condition for all. But he saw the poor as full members of the community, and Methodist societies as places where they could experience that inclusivity as a fact. All this stemmed from his sense that God, the Father of all had invited all to share in his conversation with his creation.

None of this constituted in his mind a threat to or even a challenge to Anglicanism since he encouraged all members of Methodist societies to share in the Eucharist of the local parish wherever possible. His purpose was to enliven Anglicanism with the piety of the poor and to break down the class prejudices which in his mind were a greater threat to the unity of society than many of the political and economic concerns of some of his fellow clergy. His personal generosity was notable; he gave away books, money and time with abandon and seems hardly to have been capable of passing a beggar without putting something in his hand. Indeed in order to support them he stood with them and on occasions, in Bath for instance, assisted them by begging on their behalf. His somewhat rosy view of the Early Church in Jerusalem inspired him and remained an inspiration throughout his life. It may well have been an influence in his thinking through of the distinctive development of the Methodist doctrine of perfection.

V

Concern for the Body

Concern for the body led Wesley to put together a medical handbook since at the time all had to care for their own medical needs. The theological basis of disease in all its aspects was clear to Wesley and is evidence of his conservative approach to scripture. He begins the preface to *Primitive Physic* by pointing out that God created humankind to be perfect in body, mind and spirit: in the beginning therefore he was healthy and had no need of healing.

But since man rebelled against the Sovereign of heaven and earth, how entirely is the scene changed! The incorruptible frame hath put on corruption, the immortal has put on mortality. The seeds of weakness and pain, of sickness and death, are now lodged in our inmost substance; whence a thousand disorders continually spring, even without the aid of external violence. And how is the number of these increased by every thing round about us! The heavens, the earth, and all things contained therein, conspire to punish the rebels against their Creator. The sun and moon shed unwholesome influences from above; the earth exhales poisonous damps from beneath; the beasts of the field, the birds of the air, the fishes of the sea, are in a state of hostility: yea, the food we eat, daily saps the foundation of life which cannot be sustained without it. So has the Lord of all secured the execution of his decrees, – 'Dust thou art, and unto dust thou shalt return.'[8]

The approach to scripture is hardly likely to appeal to us today but the implicit sentiments are vividly relevant and share current thinking about health. For example greed, a debilitating will to dominate creation rather than accept that we are a dimension of creation which we should have the sense to look after and poor quality food are both assumed by Wesley to be destructive of good health. But that is not all: God provides common-sense advice in scripture which would support good health.

We cannot eliminate every threat to health, cures are temporary; death is an ever-present reality. Nevertheless, there are many God-given means which we can draw on to retain or restore good health. For example, exercise, temperance and a good diet are essential for a healthy life. So is the condition of the air we breathe, the cleanliness of the home we live in and the taking of cold baths; this was very demanding advice but very relevant given the conditions of the poor workers whom Wesley met.

It is interesting that Wesley should allude to the Americans by which he means the Indians; he romantically regarded them to be still living in conformity with nature after the pattern of the Primitive Church.[9] In their culture, he affirms, religion and medicine are a unity traditionally passed from father to son: they understand their relationship with creation and know from experience what 'works'. The basis of his *Primitive Physic* is something similar. There is little in it of what we should call scientific medicine, but in one sense it is evidence-based because it states what he observed worked in the particular circumstances of a given disease.

But that is not all, for in this context too, Wesley sees things whole. 'The passions', he writes, 'have a greater influence upon health than most people are aware of'. Moreover, he adds, 'The slow and lasting passions, such as grief and hopeless love, bring on chronical diseases.'[10] Given his experience of America and his messy relationships with women, Wesley had personal experience of professional disappointment and hopeless love on which to draw! A healthy life depended upon good 'passions', keeping one's temper, controlling one's instincts and growing in self-knowledge. The Indians may not have been Christians but, as Wesley saw it, they were ready for the faith if and when they heard the gospel. Thus he concludes the preface to *Primitive Physic* with these words:

> The love of God, as it is the sovereign remedy of all
> miseries, so in particular it effectually prevents all the
> bodily disorders the passions introduce, by keeping the
> passions themselves within due bounds; and by the
> unspeakable joy and perfect calm serenity and tranquility it
> gives the mind; it becomes the most powerful of all the
> means of health and long life.[11]

Physical health, spiritual well-being and personal support were necessarily bound up with and associated indissolubly with the love of God and the acknowledgement of his presence. Learning to give attention to God through spiritual discipline will focus the body, the mind and the spirit on what is ultimately nourishing and sustaining. In this emphasis Wesley is not drawing on a narrow pietism, but on the larger traditions of Catholic and Orthodox spirituality. The support of healthcare remains a special concern of Methodist ministry.

A Passion for Education

In none of these practical concerns was Wesley the pioneer. Anglicans, Baptists and other Christians influenced by pietism were concerned for the well-being of the poor. What Wesley understood profoundly was that to have faith, to know God in Christ meant that one could not but be involved with them on a face to face basis. This was obvious to Wesley in education for which he had a real passion. He had enjoyed a good education himself at Charterhouse and retained a loyal respect for the school. However, it seems that close acquaintance with a neighbouring school – perhaps Westminster – led him to be critical of regimes which lacked, as he remembered it, sufficient emphasis upon the spiritual life and the salvation of souls. He was not an uncritical admirer of Oxford University; it was well-founded, but the tutors took their privileges more seriously than their responsibilities. When appointed tutor at Lincoln College, he undertook his pastoral responsibilities so conscientiously that he upset the authorities. A good education, he believed, involved the acquisition of good habits and self-discipline based on piety and devotion.[12]

As for learning, he himself never ceased to read extensively in many fields but most especially in theology and the spiritual life. The benefits he enjoyed he wanted to share with others and he set about the task in a thorough way. He edited and published the work of other authors in his *Christian Library*, which consisted of fifty volumes first published in 1749–1755, among which were books of theology, spiritual reading, moral instruction and history.[13] He sought without success to establish libraries in London, Bristol and Newcastle which could be consulted by preachers, and himself when he was there. For although he recognized the contribution which the unlettered could offer he realized that as the itinerant preachers moved around, their preaching and pastoral care would be enhanced by wider and regular reading.

He encouraged Sunday schools which mostly came about through local initiatives such as that of Hannah Ball in High

Wycombe whose school begun in 1769 predated Robert Raikes in Gloucester by ten years. At the beginning the schools taught Scripture, reading and other elementary subjects, but as the state took a more general interest in education in the second half of the nineteenth century, they focused more on religious education.

Perhaps the most personal of his commitments to education came with the founding in 1748 of *Kingswood School,* in Bristol, England.[14] This was to be for all Christian children, including at the very beginning both boys and girls, but from 1760s and '70s the school focused upon providing an education for the sons of itinerant preachers who might otherwise be deprived of consistent schooling. Wesley wanted above all a Christian school: the rules for it were first settled at the conference of 1748. A document published in 1749 declares that,

> Our design is, with God's assistance, to train up children, in every branch of useful learning.[15]

'Useful learning' did not mean simply the acquisition of information which would lead to a good job. Wesley's interest in education was provoked by concern for the souls of children on the grounds that early intervention is best. The focus on saving the souls of children involved ensuring that they were offered, as the 1749 document shows, a liberal education. As a student of the Enlightenment, one can hardly be surprised at the direction in which Wesley moved. Kingswood School in its early years suffered many blows from incompetent head teachers and delinquent children, much to Wesley's frustration. But the direction is clear from an advertisement in a Bristol newspaper in December 1752 by the then headmaster, James Rouquet.

> Whereas it has been long complained of, that Children generally spend seven, eight and ten Years in learning only two or three Languages; and that together with these, they learn such Vices as probably they never unlearn more:
>
> **This is to give Notice**
> That in the Forest of *King's-Wood* near BRISTOL, in a good clean air a BOARDING – SCHOOL is now

opened, wherein are taught, at 14l. (£14) *per annum* — *English, French, Latin, Greek, Hebrew, History, Geography, Chronology, Rhetoric, Logic, Ethics; Geometry, Physics;* together with *Writing* in all the useful Hands; *Arithmetic,* Vulgar, Decimal and Instrumental; *Merchants' Accompts* by Single and Double Entry; *Trigonometry,* Plain and Spherical; *Surveying* and *Mapping* of land; *Gauging* in all its Parts; *Mensuration* of all Superficies, Solids, *Etc.,* at much less Expense of Time than usual: Where particular Care is also taken of the Morals of the Children, that they may be train'd up at once to LEARNING and VIRTUE.[16]

This is some ambition! Quite apart from the marvelously generous curriculum, the notice embodies a unity of knowledge and virtue which grounds the theological perspective.

At the Bristol Conference of 1756 the Rules of the Society and the Rules of Kingswood School were read over and considered one by one: 'all were convinced that they were agreeable to Scripture and reason.'[17] We glimpse here the coherence of theology, scripture, moral perspective, reason and experience which demonstrate Wesley's approach and the subsequent tradition of Methodist theological enquiry. Michael Oakeshott talks of education in an analogous way.

Education in its most general significance may be recognized as a specific transaction which may go on between the generations of human beings in which newcomers to the scene are initiated into the world they are to inhabit.[18]

From the point of view of Methodist theology, the conversation between the generations must include conversation about God and with God which has a rich, illuminating and stimulating history without which the opportunity to mature as free persons will be hampered, if not actually denied. Oakeshott goes on to say that education must first ask the question, 'What is the character of the world which a human newcomer is to inhabit?'[19] The Christian response is that it is a world characterized by the presence of God, Creator, Redeemer and Sustainer.

Concern for education was not confined to Britain. Wherever Methodist missionaries preached the gospel whether in Africa, the West Indies, the South Pacific, they set about the provision of education and health care. North America provides the outstanding example. Methodist societies began to flourish in America from the 1760s and received an enormous boost with the arrival from England of Francis Asbury who had responded to an appeal from Wesley at the Conference of 1771 for volunteers to go to America. Asbury was inspired with a passion to bring the gospel to the American people. He understood intuitively the culture of a people who were on the move and created an itinerant system to serve them.

When in 1784 Dr Thomas Coke arrived as Wesley's emissary to discuss the future of Methodism in America, a Kingswood School in America was high on the agenda. The school opened near Baltimore in 1787 and initially flourished but was destroyed by fire in 1795. Asbury could not face the difficulties of starting all over again and his energy was focused in any case on preaching the gospel and by his own example supporting the growing number of itinerant preachers who accompanied the people trekking westward. Coke did try again but his second attempt was likewise destroyed by fire.

The passion for education is an integral expression of Methodist theological enterprise: saving souls is indelibly associated with education and health care. Universities and Colleges of Liberal Education affiliated to the Methodist Board of Higher Education and Ministry now number over one hundred in America. Methodist commitment to education continues: most recently in 1992 the United Methodist Church of America founded the African University in Mutare, Zimbabwe which has Faculties of Agriculture, Health Care, Education and Humanities and most particularly also, a faculty of Theology and an Institute of Peace Leadership and Governance. The University embodies the vision of God's presence in Christ in seeking to meet the local need of food, health, education, peace and good government.

The vital importance of holding together Knowledge and Virtue is obvious as Aquinas taught and Wesley affirmed. All stems from the profound desire to love God, follow Christ and save souls – language which is all too uncommon these days in the public discourse of Methodists.

Charles Wesley gives voice to this perspective in these two hymns.

Jesus, I fain would find
Thy zeal for God in me,
Thy yearning pity for mankind,
Thy burning charity.

In me thy Spirit dwell;
In me thy mercies move:
So shall the fervour of my zeal
Be thy pure flame of love.[20]

It is a passion for God inspired by Jesus and given life by the Spirit, which will enable the faithful believer to love others in Christ's name even as he knows himself to have been loved. But it will require, as he knows full well, hard work if he is to embody the love of God, retain a sense of God's presence in himself, shun evil and live to God's glory.

Be it my only wisdom here,
To serve the Lord with filial fear,
With loving gratitude;
Superior sense may I display
By shunning every evil way,
And walking in the good.

O may I still from sin depart;
A wise and understanding heart,
Jesus, to me be given!
And let me through thy Spirit know
To glorify my God below,
And find my way to heaven.[21]

Nine references to Scripture here, just to make sure that we know on what ground he stands!

VII

The Servant Community

The Methodist Church is a Servant Community and Methodist theology a servant theology: the latter is a more informative term than practical theology because it holds together our service of God's creation and our attention to God the redemptive Creator. The ultimate ground of Methodist Faith is God; God in Trinity, Father, Son and Holy Spirit. It is God first to whom Wesley and Methodists give authority, and only secondly to the Bible, and to Jesus because of what we believe they reveal of the God on whom our attention is focused. God is Creator of all that is and has exercised his power to commit himself to work for the perfection of his creation: he will not let us go. It is because Wesley chose to give God authority, that he felt empowered to serve the needs of all people, especially the poor, the outcast, the sick and the prisoner.

Nothing remains the same, however, for any length of time: all is subject to flux and change. In Wesley's lifetime the world began to shift dramatically. He remarked upon the tendency of those who became wealthy through thrift, sobriety and self-discipline – or who at least enjoyed freedom from anxiety about their personal circumstances – to find comfort in attention to the things of this world rather than in their love of God, their attention to the spiritual life and the service of others. There is one world created by God; one family of humankind: all are loved and nourished by God's abounding grace. A servant theology will be shaped by attending to the particular needs which are identified in the light of the vision which attention to God stimulates. The vision of the world which is promoted by giving attention to God is inclusive and subtle.

Wesley's concerns continue to this day; the poor are ever with us and education remains a vital dimension of life if humankind is to flourish as does the world's need to become aware of God's redeemed presence. But to what now is our attention drawn? Inequality? Certainly, but it is such a vague term that precision is necessary before it becomes something on which we can act. Perhaps something as essential and simple as the availability of water would focus our minds. It is necessary to all life; competition for it is a far greater threat to the peace of the world over the next twenty years than the failure of energy supply. Has our servant theology anything to say which would inform our wills and affectionate concern for the future of God's creation? What can the Servant Church offer the world?

VIII

Conclusion

Faith is belief in action.[22] God is indivisibly Being and Doing. In the following chapter we look to the God who in creating has committed himself to conversation with his creation, to the doctrine of prevenient grace which inspired John Wesley and to the much misunderstood doctrine of perfection.

Chapter 4

The Presence of God

I

Introduction

Methodist theology takes God seriously and therefore with equal seriousness the world of God's creation which Jesus calls his Church to serve in the power of the Spirit. Wesley preached that the ultimate goal of discipleship was the perfect love of God and of neighbours. He thought through his theology in order to discern what this might mean for the world, the individual believer and the Church.

Tillich argued that theology must serve the needs of the Church.

A theological system is supposed to satisfy two basic needs: the statement of the truth of the Christian message and the interpretation of this truth for every new generation. Theology moves back and forth between these two poles, the eternal truth of its foundation and the temporal situation in which the eternal truth must be received.[1]

This is in principle what Methodist theology is intent upon doing: holding together in one enquiry the revelation of himself which God vouchsafes in Christ and the circumstances in which human beings find themselves in the world. But it begins with God.

God, Tillich said, is the ground of our being. Though not a term with which Wesley would have been familiar, it is I believe one with which he would have been comfortable. It is consistent with the doctrine of prevenient grace which is an essential ingredient of Wesley's theological position and deeply embedded in subsequent Methodist theology. It underpins the Methodist belief that salvation is open to all, not only the predestined few.

II

The Nature and Presence of God

The dynamic centre of Methodist theological reflection is God, Father, Son and Holy Spirit. It is the Trinitarian God who inspires Wesley's passion for souls and on whom he is focused. Who is this God?

God is who God is. He is free, unconstrained by anything outside himself which in theological terminology is taken to mean that God brought the world into being 'out of nothing'. God is only limited in what he wants to do by who he is, that is by his own nature of love. God in creating does what he wants to do, in accordance with his own nature. So when thinking about God as Creator, we can see that the creation is an expression of the inherent desire of the love within the Godhead to make a world with which he is in relation and always will be. God was neither forced by a power beyond his control to create the world, nor is he limited by its materiality in the extent to which it can grow in response to his love.

In order that the creation could experience a quality of life in its own creaturely terms analogous to that which God enjoyed in himself, God gave human beings the opportunity to recognize the true nature of the world in which they were set and the freedom to know and respond to his living presence with them. God has made possible a relationship with him which when accepted and established transforms the sense human beings have of themselves. They emerge from the illusion of being outsiders in a world which is foreign to them into the reality that they are at home in the world where God is irremovably present and to which he has committed himself. No true account of human experience would be complete which ignored the fact that the world is a creation and not a happenstance. Indeed, a full understanding of the freedom of humankind to enter into relationship with God leads to the realization that they share with God the task of bringing the creation to perfection. In a profound sense, the process is one of divinization: we become one with God, though always distinct from the Creator in our creatureliness. The relationship of God and the world remains eternally dynamic.

Theology, for John Wesley, was intended to transform life. Always in the service of presenting the gospel, theology was to underwrite the proclamation of the grace of God given in Jesus Christ for the redemption of all people.[2]

The gospel was God's good news, not an unaided insight of human philosophical speculation. That the world of God's creation could receive the whole of what it is for God to be God without destroying the creatureliness of the creation was made clear in the person of Jesus Christ whom Methodist theology affirms, according to the orthodox position, to be both human and divine. We enjoy the God-given freedom to transform the world after the pattern which God has revealed in the person of Jesus Christ. The freedom to love God and the world belongs to all. Hence Wesley was utterly persuaded of the mistake of predestination as presented by Calvin and the Reformed tradition.

III

Wesley's Arminianism

Arminius (1560–1609) was a Dutch Reformed theologian, whose study of the Epistle to the Romans led him to challenge the Calvinist doctrine of predestination. He took the view that the authority of God was consistent with human freewill. Jesus died for all and not just for the elect and so, in his opinion, the doctrine of predestination was contrary to scripture. Wesley stood firmly within this Arminian tradition.[3]

'Arminian' was often a term of abuse in Wesley's time so much so that he felt he had to defend himself against unjustified accusations in a brief paper on the topic.[4]

To say, 'This man is an Arminian,' has the same effect on many hearers, as to say, 'This is a mad dog.'

Wesley identifies five errors popularly associated with Arminianism.

(1) That they deny original sin; (2) That they deny justification by faith; (3) That they deny absolute predestination;
(4) That they deny the grace of God to be irresistible; and
(5) That they affirm, a believer may fall from grace.

But, Wesley says, Arminianism neither denies original sin nor
justification by faith; on the contrary it affirms both, as did Wesley.
On the other hand, with regard to the further three charges, he
agrees that Arminianism asserts the freedom of humankind to
accept or to reject the salvation which God offers in Christ and
even to fall from grace through failure to live in faith. He goes on
to urge sensibly that the term 'Calvinist' should never be used as a
term of reproach since calling people names contributes nothing
to public understanding.

Wesley's lack of sympathy with the position of Calvin and the
Reformed tradition is based on the fact that it simply made no
sense to him in the light of scripture and his understanding of
God.[5] The Reformers' conception of God as unbending, demanding, determining, punitive, as unresponsive to the human condition
was false to Scripture, tradition, experience and reason. Such a
view of God, Wesley believed, was denied by Jesus' life, teaching,
sacrificial death, resurrection and ascension which expressed the
fullness of God's presence with the world that he was making.

The theological argument in the sixteenth century precipitated
divisions in the Church: in fact the confusion involved more than
debate about doctrine, about God's relationship with the world,
the nature of the Church, the authority of the Pope, the interpretation of scripture and the extent or not of human freewill. It was
a theological controversy which impacted widely on the political
life of Europe, not simply on the doctrinal positions of the Protestant Churches, through the political expediency of the princes
of the German states who in their own interests were opposed to
the authority of Rome. Calvin in Geneva, Bucer in Strasburg,
Zwingli and Bullinger in Zurich and Luther in Saxony had their
overlapping if conflicting perspectives but each influenced the
religious traditions of their respective states.

The controversy continued to rage in the seventeenth and
eighteenth centuries and divided theological opinion in the British

Isles too. Given his Arminian convictions Wesley could not side-step the issues with the consequence that he was brought into inevitable conflict with Calvinists throughout his life. It had, of course, a particular impact in Evangelical circles: Wesley had come across the doctrine of predestination both in Oxford and in America. But it was most particularly in reaction to his experience of the Moravians with their quietism and to George Whitefield's public espousal of Calvinism in his preaching that Wesley found himself having to defend his Arminianism.

Calvin believed God to be omnipotent and omniscient, in the sense that he was in control of all things and therefore knew and determined the future which could not change or be altered in any way. At the fall, Adam disregarded the will of God and stained by sin, he and his progeny lost their innocence; they stood condemned before God in total depravity. However, God had foreseen the disobedience of humankind from the beginning of creation and taken steps graciously to save some whose number and names God knew from all eternity. The rest of the human race was destined for eternal damnation in the torments of hell.

As a trained lawyer and a shrewd politician, Calvin's conception of God was as Just Judge and Governor. An omnipotent and omniscient God could neither make legal mistakes, nor misjudge his political authority. Since all lived in sin God's condemnation was just. None of those who were sentenced by their own sin had any right to complain, reason to question or power to resist God's judgement. No appeal was reasonable because they knew themselves condemned by their own sinfulness. In any case, there was no higher court to which they could appeal; God was the absolute monarch, the ultimate source of authority and justice. Moreover, the Elect could not fall from grace since irrespective of their merits or demerits their salvation was guaranteed. The will of God is absolute: his judgement final.

The position is unambiguously stated in the Presbyterian Westminster Confession (1647) quoted by Wesley.[6]

God from all eternity did unchangeably ordain whatsoever comes to pass.

By the decree of God, for the manifestation of his glory, some men and angels are predestinated unto everlasting life and others fore-ordained to everlasting death.

These angels and men thus predestinated and fore-ordained are particularly and unchangeably designed, and their number so certain and definite, that it cannot be either increased or diminished.

Those of mankind that are predestinated unto life, God, before the foundation of the world, hath chosen in Christ unto everlasting glory, without any foresight of faith or good works. The rest of mankind God was pleased, for the glory of his sovereign power over his creatures, to pass by and to ordain them to dishonor and wrath.

Wesley found this wholly abhorrent, contrary to Scripture and to his experience. As far as he was concerned God as revealed by Jesus Christ was not a God who predestined and 'unchangeably designed' some to heavenly bliss and others to hell, 'without any foresight of faith or good works'. Indeed a God who denied his creatures all happiness and virtue 'from all eternity' was no God at all and simply unbelievable. God was not an automaton and had not created automata. Wesley preached the contrary. God had graciously chosen to share the freedom he enjoyed in himself in the unity of the Trinity with his creatures so as to give them the choice of salvation.[7] Humankind is in this sense made in the image of God.

Methodist theology continues to preach the gospel in the light of the Arminian conviction that humankind is free.[8] Thus, for example, Richard Watson (1781–1833), the most influential Methodist theologian on both sides of the Atlantic in the first years after Wesley's death, put together in his *Theological Institutes*, a first attempt to systematize Methodist theology.[9] In it he declared that while God's sovereignty was undeniable, his grace was not irresistible. But God exercised his sovereign grace so as to enable and inspire human responsibility. Thomas Ware (1758–1842), a widely travelled preacher and leader in early American Methodism was quite sure that Christ died for all. William Burt Pope (1822–1903), claimed that while God is only known through revelation, apart from a God-given capacity to discern divine truth, God's revelation would be unintelligible and lack all redemptive power.

The question came alive again for Karl Barth, in his despair after the chaos of the First World War; he rejected the current liberal inclination of theology and declared God's judgement on human society and human culture. The only hope for humankind lay in the absolute freedom of God and his gracious revelation of himself in Christ. Wesley was no Barthian before Barth, but while not condemning all human culture and claiming the relevance of reason to theological enquiry, he did share with him an absolute confidence in God's freedom to be himself. Later Methodist theologians such as Scott Lidgett (1854–1953) took up this position: precisely because God is a God of love, God could not but make a world of opportunity and hope in which humankind could know him and his loving presence, choose to recognize him, follow him and be freed to live in love and harmony with other persons and the whole of creation. Far from living in fear of God, they could live in an affectionate family relationship with him – Lidgett embraced the image of God as Father in order to ground his insight in ordinary human experience – with one another and with the world.[10] Of course, one lives on the edge of fear in the weak sense that one lives by faith not by knowledge, but that simply means that in the face of temptation one has to confirm frequently one's decision to accept the freedom one has in God's good creation – and one is free to do so.

The debate is alive today given the political, moral and social perspectives which threaten world destruction. Armageddon, some believe – including some who potentially wield extraordinary power – is just around the corner and political, military, economic and environmental choices must be made with that in mind. Who says theology is irrelevant to public life!

IV

The Trinity

The dynamic centre of Methodist theology is God conceived as the loving community of the Father, the Son and the Holy Spirit.

In his sermon 'On the Trinity', Wesley is clear where he stands. The Trinity, he says, 'enters into the very heart of Christianity: It lies at the heart of all vital religion'.[11] He places it at the centre of worship, of the experience of God and of his ecclesiology. Charles Wesley produced a collection of 182 *Hymns on the Trinity* in 1767 which confirms the centrality of this theme to Methodist theology and worship.

Hail, holy, holy, holy Lord,
Whom One in Three we know;
By all thy heavenly host adored,
By all thy Church below.

One undivided Trinity
With triumph we proclaim;
Thy universe is full of thee,
And speaks thy glorious name.

Thee, holy Father, we confess;
Thee, holy Son, adore;
Thee, Spirit of truth and holiness,
We worship evermore.

The incommunicable right,
Almighty God, receive,
Which angel choirs, and saints in light,
And saints embodied give.

Three Persons equally divine
We magnify and love;
And both the choirs ere long shall join
To sing thy praise above.

Hail, holy, holy, holy Lord
(Our heavenly song shall be),
Supreme, essential One adored
In co-eternal Three![12]

Remarkably notwithstanding this evidence, Frank Whaling, for example, has claimed that the Trinity was secondary in Wesley's theology to more fundamental doctrines, 'prevenient grace, justification by faith, assurance, sanctification and perfect love'.[13] But on what could these 'more fundamental' doctrines be grounded, if not a well-developed doctrine of the Trinity?

It is true that despite the centrality of the Trinity to Wesleyan theology little attention was paid to it for the first two hundred years of Methodist history. Richard Watson, for example, pointed to the moral agency of man as presumptive evidence for the existence of God and to revelation as the source of knowledge of the Trinitarian nature of God. However, while it is clear that he accepted the Trinity, his emphasis was on revelation as a source of knowledge rather than on the importance of the Trinity as the ground of Christian Faith. John Miley (1813–1895) and Thomas Summers (1812–1882), offer systematic theologies, but the Trinity does not grab their attention – discussion of the doctrine occupies little more than 1 per cent of the text in either case.[14] Borden Parker Bowne (1847–1910), was keen to relate his theology to the wider philosophical world. He followed Lotze in the belief that feeling rather than mere intellectualism was the key to understanding the deeply personal character of what it is to be human. The human capacity for personal relationships revealed the true nature of humanity with implications for the whole created order: it provided evidence, he believed, for the existence of a personal Creator God. But despite, or perhaps because of his underlying commitment to personalism, a view which dominated theology in America until the mid-twentieth century, there was, surprisingly I think, no serious interest in the doctrine of the Persons of the Trinity *per se*.

The neglect of the Trinity within Methodist theology which this marks is coincident with centuries of growing prosperity. Prosperity was equated with success, which was in turn believed to be the consequence of individual effort and the outcome of competition. The personal focus of much theologizing with its emphasis on individual salvation may have given mistaken credence to the view that prosperity was morally justified and the God-given reward of individual faithfulness. Yet, of course, the Christian understanding of the personal is not at all individualistic; it exists only in community. Persons flourish in friendship at its deepest and most real; they depend upon courtesy, mutual commitment and love. These are features of human life that illuminate a limited grasp of what it is for God to be Trinitarian.

Methodism was not exceptional in neglecting the Trinity: it was largely neglected in all Protestant theology until Karl Barth. Within Methodism it was Geoffrey Wainwright who re-affirmed the centrality of the doctrine to Methodist thinking about God. Wainwright is the British-born Professor of Christian Theology in the Divinity School at Duke University who published his influential systematic theology in 1980.[15] He shared in and encouraged a burgeoning interest in Wesleyan theology, and like Wesley himself was influenced by wide reading in Protestant, Orthodox and Catholic theology. His perspective is grounded in the experience of worship, especially in the Eucharist where, he says quite rightly, attention is actually focused on God as Trinity. The Persons of the Godhead are bound together in a mutuality of love which overflows in creation, redemption and sustaining creativity. Believers share in the divine love in Eucharistic worship which underpins and informs the possibility and indeed the potential perfection of human affectionate living in relationship to God, one another and the whole creation.

V

God the Father, Revealed in Jesus

God is the origin, source, ground of being and the Creator who accepts responsibility for all that is. He is, Wesley preached, the father of Jesus Christ, the Father of all and therefore, 'Our Father'. Jesus is the Word of the Father, through whom all things were made, so that what characterizes the personal relationship of Jesus and the Father whom he reveals, underpins the whole relationship of Creator and creation. Nothing is outside God's love, or exclusive of his presence. Raymond E. Brown, the distinguished Roman Catholic scholar, entitles Jesus' Last Discourse in his commentary on St John's Gospel; *Jesus is the way to the Father for those who believe in him*.[16] St. John puts powerful words in Jesus' mouth:

I am the way and the truth and the life: no one comes to the Father except through me. If you men really knew me, then you would recognize my Father too. From now on you do know Him and have seen Him.[17]

They sum up Wesley's approach. Jesus is not the way *to* the Truth, but the way *of* Truth to the Father. There is no fundamental distinction between the moral and the revelatory aspects of Jesus implicit in Jesus' claim to be 'the way': St John holds them together, as does Wesley. Belief in Jesus as the revelation of the Father means behaving as a son, and walking in the footsteps of Jesus who is the Son. Philip's plea to be shown the Father expresses the Methodist desire to know God.

> Philip said to him, 'Lord, show us the Father, and we will be satisfied.' Jesus said to him. 'Have I been with you all this time Philip, and you still do not know me? Whoever has seen me has seen the Father. How can you say, "Show us the Father"? Do you not believe that I am in the Father and the Father is in me? The words which I say to you I do not speak on my own; but the Father who dwells in me does his works. Believe me that I am in the Father and the Father is in me; but if you do not then believe me because of the works themselves. Very truly, I tell you, the one who believes in me will also do the works that I do and, in fact, will do greater works than these, because I am going to the Father. I will do whatever you ask in my name, so that the Father may be glorified in the Son.'[18]

Jesus and God are one, God is his father. His humanity finds its fulfillment in his relationship with God his father. But implicit in Jesus' recognition of God as his father, is that all are included. Thus when his disciples ask him to teach them how to pray, Jesus explains that they must assume a relationship with God their Father. We rightly know the prayer as *The Lord's Prayer*. The profound point is that Our Lord asks his disciples – that is in principle all Christians, and in them all people – to join in praying with him and in him; he is not simply giving them words to pray. 'When you pray, say, "Our Father in heaven, hallowed be your name." We hardly ever, it seems to me, when we pray this prayer grasp just what we are saying, and by our saying also what we are in fact doing. We are in and with Christ assuming our filial relation with God our Father and including in our prayer all creation.'[19]

That word 'Our' is most powerful; when we pray *Our Father* and recognize the implication of what we are saying, the words are transformative of our experience. They bring to mind the truly divine dimensions of the world in which we live. When that is grasped, there is no limit to the authority on which they can call, 'so that the Father may be glorified in the Son', which means to make others aware of what they themselves are invited to understand, that God is present in Jesus Christ reconciling the world to himself.

St Paul makes a similar point when he says in writing to the Galatians, that they have through Christ been freed from their former guardianship under the law as minors and given the full liberty of children 'by adoption'.

> But when the fullness of time had come, God sent his Son, born of a woman, born under the law, in order to redeem those who were under the law, so that we might receive adoption as children. And because you are children, God has sent the Spirit of his Son into our hearts, crying 'Abba! Father!' So you are no longer a slave but a child, and if a child then also an heir, through God.[20]

The self-imposed law on which they are hooked blinds them to the freedom of God's law, into which all enter as soon as they realize their adoption into the family as sons. John Wesley understood this very well in his several paraphrases of the The Lord's Prayer.[21] 'Father of all', he writes, and means it.

> Father of all, whose powerful voice
> Called forth this universal frame,
> Whose mercies over all rejoice,
> Through endless ages still the same;
> Thou by thy word upholdest all;
> Thy bounteous love to all is showed;
> Thou hear'st thy every creature's call,
> And fillest every mouth with good.
>
> In heaven thou reign'st enthroned in light,
> Nature's expanse beneath thee spread;

Earth, air, and sea before thy sight,
And hell's deep gloom, are open laid.
Wisdom, and might, and love are thine;
Prostrate before thy face we fall,
Confess thine attributes divine,
And hail the sovereign Lord of all.

Thee, sovereign Lord, let all confess
That moves in earth, or air, or sky,
Revere thy power, thy goodness bless,
Tremble before thy piercing eye;
All ye who owe to him your birth,
In praise your every hour employ;
Jehovah reigns! Be glad, O earth,
And shout ye morning stars, for joy.

Disciples pray not on behalf of the faithful as if they were the exclusive society, but on behalf of all people, as the hymn makes plain.

Thy bounteous love to all is showed;
Thou hear'st thy every creature's call,
And fillest every mouth with food.

Charles Wesley makes a similar claim in this fine hymn.[22]

Father of me and all mankind,
And all the hosts above,
Let every understanding mind
Unite to praise thy love;

To know thy nature and thy name,
One God in Persons Three;
And glorify the great I AM
Through all eternity.

Thy kingdom come, with power and grace,
To every heart of man;
Thy peace, and joy, and righteousness
In all our bosoms reign.

Jesus knows God as his father, and by the wholeness of his being and living, reveals God to be my father and the Father of all mankind. Awareness of the personal and the universal nature of God's unlimited love for the created order and for humankind is inherent in Wesley's preaching and Methodist hymnology.

VI

God Alive in the Holy Spirit

St Paul points the Christians in Rome to their freedom in Christ and the consequent indwelling of the Spirit which makes them children of God.

> For all who are led by the Spirit and children of God. For you did not receive a spirit of slavery to fall back into fear, but you have received a spirit of adoption. When we cry, 'Abba! Father! It is that very Spirit bearing witness with our spirit that we are children of God, and if children, then heirs, heirs of God and joint heirs with Christ – if, in fact, we suffer with him so that we may also be glorified with him'.[23]

The inheritance into which the Christian enters with Christ is the future heavenly peace. The hope of sharing in his glory is secured by Christ's sacrifice which reveals the ineradicable, gracious and unmerited presence of God with his creation. We may share his glory in the sense that we too, with Christ, may live in the presence of God for ever.

The Holy Spirit given in the sacrament of baptism, which must be in the name of the Trinity, confirms God's covenantal relationship with humankind from the moment of creation. It promises the hope of salvation through sharing in dying and rising with Christ. The witness of the spirit is justification by faith and the assurance of God's presence. There is no such thing as inward assurance of God's presence apart from evidence of the fruit of the spirit which Wesley declares are 'love, joy, peace, long-suffering, gentleness, goodness'. In this way too, Wesley holds together Jesus' revelation of the Father, and the living out of faith in a spiritually aware 'moral' life.

VII

Prevenient Grace

It is important to recognize that the first gifts of the Spirit given to the penitent sinner are thankfulness, joy and love. The demands of Methodist faith were not, and are not, over-bearing; neither do they demand the abandonment of personal initiative. On the contrary when they are properly understood they are simply delightful and personally fulfilling. St. Augustine in his *Confessions* wrote,

> Thou awakest us to delight in Thy praise; for Thou madest us for Thyself, and our heart is restless, until it repose in Thee. Grant me, Lord, to know and understand which is first, to call on Thee or to praise Thee? and, again, to know Thee or to call on Thee? For who can call on Thee, not knowing Thee?[24]

This is what God does, because this is who God is: Being and Doing are one in God. Wesley understood what it was to have a restless heart and find that his repose lay in God alone. What is more, he discerned with utter clarity that but for the grace of God he would not have been able to call upon God. Wesley was familiar with the Anglican Book of Common Prayer and would have regularly prayed the Second Collect for Peace.

> O God, who art the author of peace and lover of concord, in knowledge of whom standeth our eternal life, whose service is perfect freedom; Defend us thy humble servants in all assaults of our enemies; that we, surely trusting in thy defence, may not fear the power of any adversaries, through the might of Jesus Christ our Lord. Amen.

Wesley would have understood what he meant when he prayed, 'whose service is perfect freedom', for what God required of a person he granted the means to perform. That is expressed in the doctrine of prevenient grace, a dimension of theological concern which Wesley thought profoundly important. Prevenient grace is not something additional to or 'other' than God; it is (or should one say, 'he is'?) actually the Triune God, given in creation, incarnate in Christ, powerfully present in the Spirit, working to bring all humankind to full awareness of the salvific character of the world which God invites them to enjoy.

How else could the believer have become aware of God apart from the stimulus of God himself? How could God be true to his own loving nature if he was not irrevocably committed to his creation?

VIII

The Doctrine of Perfection

That each person was the subject of God's love implied for Wesley that each person could be saved utterly. The inheritance into which all mankind was called in Christ was the perfection of existence in communion with God, Father, Son and Holy Spirit. The creature, while remaining true to his own creaturely nature was called to share the life of the Creator. In this divinization lay his perfection.

The doctrine of perfection is a frequently misunderstood aspect of Wesley's theology.[25] It has therefore often been ignored and neglected.[26] A contemporary scholar remarks that 'John Wesley's doctrine of Christian perfection is at best a dead letter and at worst a source of political delusion among contemporary Methodists.'[27] Indeed its slide into silence in theological discussion and as the subject of sermons in Methodism in nineteenth-century America, led to the compensating emergence of the Holiness Churches, and latterly to the rise of the Church of the Nazarenes and of Pentecostalism. Yet the perspective of faith and love opened up and celebrated in the doctrine of perfection is at the centre of Methodist theology. Properly understood, it is a core theological insight of Christian theology as a whole to which Wesley gave renewed attention.

Wesley straightly dismissed in his sermon on *Christian Perfection* any suggestion that 'perfect' meant 'faultless'. 'For Christians, therefore, are not so perfect as to be free either from ignorance or error. We may, thirdly, add: nor from infirmities.' He goes on to deny that they will be free from temptation.

The doctrine of perfection is not particular to Wesley. He was influenced by the Eastern tradition of theology as found for example in Macarius (fourth–fifth century), and by the Anglican tradition of 'holiness' in the writings of John Jewell (1522–1571), and Jeremy Taylor (1613–1667). Perfection for Wesley implies the possibility that, as part of the process of sanctification a person may come to love God completely and may be certain

> *in a present moment,* of the fullness of one's love for God and
> neighbor, as this love has been initiated and fulfilled by
> God's gifts of faith, hope and love.[28]

Albert Outler, a major figure in the revival of Wesleyan studies in the second half of the twentieth century, failed to recognize that the doctrine of perfection lies at the heart of Wesley's theology. Like many others before and since, Outler appreciated the importance of the search for holiness in the Wesleyan tradition, but reduced it to love of God and love of neighbour thus sweeping aside the full demands of holiness as Wesley saw them. Love of God and love of neighbour are qualities of the Christian life, but they are by themselves too easily reduced to an appeal for personal moral endeavour and political action to secure the common good. Not that these should be dismissed as irrelevant: but as a summary of Wesley's attitude to faithful living and holiness they are woefully inadequate.

The reason for this is that they do not take account of the wholeness of the Wesleyan understanding of God and of the world, or indeed of Wesley's respect for the words of Jesus according to the Sermon on the Mount in Matthew's Gospel. 'Be perfect, therefore, as you heavenly Father is perfect.'[29] This shocking command of Jesus brings one up short, but it has no meaning unless he believed that it was possible for his disciples to obey it. Following his Lord, Wesley believed that such obedience was possible and that perfection was therefore within the grasp of every person of faith. Wesley is not alone in taking this position. It is a feature of the ascetic spirituality of the Jesuit, Jean Pierre de Caussade (1675–1751) in his *Abandonment to Divine Providence*.[30] The question is not whether it is possible to be perfect as our Father in heaven is perfect but rather what it means to seek perfection, to be perfect and perhaps above all, how we can cope with the experience of discouragement in the face of what one believes to be failure.

De Caussade is clear about this. God's commitment to humankind, each and every one of us, is of himself in loving kindness. Therefore one can presume that in every circumstance in which one finds oneself God is with us and that it is therefore possible to know God's love and do God's will. In finding it and doing it, there lies perfection. As Wesley wrote in his sermon on perfection, it is possible to know and be perfect in one's love of God and neighbour *in the present moment*. The problem is that pride leads us to exaggerate our responsibilities and bite off more than we can chew: this is an aspect of our sinfulness. In some circumstances ambition and enterprise are undoubtedly desirable qualities, but for the most part we should focus on what is immediately within our grasp. Thus while world peace is a fine target for every citizen to aim at, working at peace within one's family, with one's friends and in a local church is something of fundamental value and achievable.

In this sense, Wesley was convinced that with God's grace anything was achievable. But the believer needs to be reminded of this regularly or the experience of daily living and the condition of the world in which he is set will gradually undermine his faith in the God who has justified him. Wesley's approach to this was local and organizational. Each person needed to be encouraged not simply by the worship of the Church, but by weekly class meetings overseen by faithful leaders and related to a pattern of scrupulous personal examination, bible study and prayer. These were not considered to be extras for the especially holy but necessary for all Methodists if their desire for perfection was to be fulfilled. The open concern of faith for the world, particularly for the poor, was expressed by the penny contribution asked for in charity.

IX

Conclusion

The God on whom Methodist theology is focused is the Trinitarian God of the Christian tradition. He, Creator, Redeemer and Sustainer of all that is, has committed himself to fulfil his purpose in creation. Jesus Christ reveals that God is not only *his* father but the father of all people who are invited to address him in the conversation of prayer by the familiar term 'Abba', – 'Daddy'! All are invited to enter into the inheritance promised in the covenant which God established with his people in creation. The promise of freedom from the illusion of failure and the consequence of the presumed separation from God, which we call sin, is continually present in God's prevenient grace, the personal presence in the creation of the Divine Trinity, Father, Son and Holy Spirit. In his prevenient grace God awakens human persons to realize their true nature and enables their response, which leads to the acceptance of forgiveness, the enjoyment of the fruits of the Spirit and participation in the Triune life.

Chapter 5

A Revolutionary Gospel

I

Introduction

The gospel is God's; in fact the good news which in faith we enjoy and proclaim is God; in order to preach creatively we have, therefore, to do our best to come to terms with the God whose good news we proclaim. For Methodism God is all in all. It is to him that we devote our attention in order to draw on his strength: he is Creator, Redeemer and ever present Spirit. He revolutionizes our lives.

John Wesley reminded the Church of his time of four things. First, human life will only be fulfilling when it is lived in the company of God. Secondly, God is not an absentee landlord, nor an unjust steward; he is the encouraging, sustaining and lively presence whose hand is outstretched waiting to be taken by all who seek him. Thirdly, God and human being are not separated by an unbridgeable gulf, but united in Christ. Fourthly, it is therefore possible to know God, to take his hand and to live a fulfilling life. This truth, a profound source of joy and peace, is deeply rooted in Methodist experience and in process of being worked out in Methodist theology.

I said above that Wesley *reminded* the church of his time of these dimensions of the Faith, because his perception is by no means original. He believed that he was recalling at a time of political, theological, intellectual and moral confusion, the central truths of the faith. He did not believe that he was announcing anything new; but Wesley was not looking for something new. He was seeking the way of truth; that is, he was looking for God. And when he found him, his joy stemmed not from the conviction that he would never let God go, but from the deeper conviction that whatever happened God would never let him go. The truth that lay behind that conviction came from the realization that God had been present with him from the beginning but he had not noticed. Had that not been so, God would not have been there to be recognized. In contrasting ways this is at the heart of the gospel. St. Augustine as we have seen, Origen and St. Thomas had built their theologies on the same conviction. St. Thomas returned to the point in his sermons, commentaries and in the *Summa*. But for God's eternal loving presence we would be lost in a world we could never completely hope to love, and in which we could never be ourselves.

> No conversion to God unless God turn to us. To be turned to God is to be ready for grace – you must open your eyes to be ready to see: this we cannot do without the free help of God arousing us.[1]

The fact that Wesley's perspective was not original makes it no less revolutionary. To begin to grasp – however meagerly – the dynamic implications of God's loving presence turns the world upside down; nothing can ever be the same again. For the fact is that when in the light of the revelation of God in Christ one has glimpsed and begun to form a clearer idea of the nature of God and God's relationship with his creation, our own understanding of the world and our experience of it is also revolutionized. The fact is that one can be oneself for the first time. Like the Prodigal Son we come to ourselves when we remember our relationship with our Father, and decide to return home. It is what we mean by conversion.

We accept that not only does the universe (which includes humankind) have its origin in God, but God is by his living presence continuing to make it and will always be doing so. God is there – no, better to say, God is here – for us and with us. Nothing that any individual or community has done or could do, will bring about God's absence, though by one's misdirected thinking or misguided behaviour one may lose, fail to appreciate or be led to ignore the presence of God in one's own or in the community's life.

Some Implications

Confidence in God's prevenient grace has creative implications for Methodist theology and practice because it makes it plain that faith is not based on fear of God but on the real experience of God's love. In worship, for example, we do not badger God for favours, or believe that we have to plead for forgiveness. On the contrary in worship, especially in the Eucharist, Methodists begin by celebrating *the fact* of God's presence in Christ, in the world and in the community of all God's people. Methodists are a thankful people: as already affirmed Methodist theology is rooted in thankfulness for God's gifts of life, health and salvation in Christ.

So in evangelism, God is always there before us and with us: the Church works with God, rather than working for God. In this as in many other ways, Methodism stands within a catholic tradition, something which surprises many Methodists but should not. For example, what Karl Rahner S. J. (1904–1984) has to say about preaching is entirely consistent with the approach of John Wesley.

> The preaching is the express awakening of what is already present in the depths of man's being, not by nature, but by grace. But it is a grace which always surrounds man, even the sinner and the unbeliever, as the inescapable setting of his existence.[2]

God anticipates us in evangelism and the preaching of the word and also in the day to day business of pastoral care; the minister is not bringing God into a situation but bearing witness to his presence. The task is to prompt persons to become aware of God in the depths of their being. In his sermon '*On Working Out Our Own Salvation*', Wesley states his firm conviction that,

> no man sins because he has not grace, but because he does not use the grace which he hath.

He goes on to affirm secondly,

> God worketh in you; therefore you must work. You must
> be 'workers together with him.' . . . otherwise he will cease
> working.[3]

No account of the world of human experience will be complete
if God is not included; for God's 'prevenient grace' (what Wesley
in this sermon calls preventing grace) is an ever-present reality.

Karl Rahner makes something of the same point. There is no
such thing as a distinction between the grace of God and God.
To be encouraged by God's grace, is to be encouraged by God.
To be called by God's grace, is to be called by God. In this way,
Rahner affirms that the order of creation and the order of redemption are the same. It is, as it were, of God's nature that he could do
no other than create redemptively; that is how he is and therefore
how he is as he gives himself to the making of the world. The
result is that there is no such thing, Rahner says, as nature *per se*.

> Our actual nature is *never* pure nature. It is a nature
> installed in a supernatural order which man can never
> leave, even as a sinner and unbeliever.[4]

Wesley would have agreed with him; as he said in the sermon
quoted above,

> . . . there is no man that is in a state of mere nature; there is
> no man, unless he has quenched the Spirit, that is wholly
> void of the grace of God.

Thomas Langford's comment on Methodist theology assumes the
same perspective.

> In sum, the task of theology is to interpret the gracious
> presence of God rightly and to apply it effectively.[5]

In a profound sense, therefore preaching is not a matter of adding
a new dimension to ordinary human experience; rather it draws
attention to the significance of ordinary human experience by

putting it in the divine context which makes sense of it. As Confucius said,

> ...a common man marvels at uncommon things; a wise
> man marvels at the commonplace.

Proclamation is the announcement of the gospel, the good news that the world in which human beings live and move and have their being is not defined by the literally natural, but includes the gracious reality of God's presence. The purpose behind the proclamation of the gospel is to awaken the hearers to this fact and to invite them to live in the real world.

III

Wider Perspectives

This revolutionary insight into the nature of God and the proclamation of the gospel has wider perspectives. First, God's gracious presence is not a private matter disclosed to the individual: it is a universal phenomenon, for every person wherever he or she is. Secondly, therefore, it is not something to be hugged to oneself silently, but to be enjoyed, shared and explored with others. It is, of course, personal; salvation can be enjoyed by each person but precisely because it is personal it is necessarily also social.

Wesley grasped this point; since God did not ration his grace (i.e. his presence), neither could the Christian Church. The Church must be welcoming, inclusive, caring and concerned not just for its 'members', but for the whole world of God's creation. Rahner is very clear about what is at stake here.

> Theology has been too long and too often bedeviled by
> the unavowed supposition that grace would be no longer
> grace if it were too generously distributed by the love
> of God.[6]

As if humankind could police the freedom of God to be who God is, and restrict his grace by the self-righteous dimensions of human justice! The fact is that since there is no distinction between God and God's grace the thought that God's grace can be limited is impossible.

> Our whole spiritual life is lived in the realm of the salvific
> will of God, of his prevenient grace . . . [7]

Thirdly, the end to which we are called and which is affirmed by the normality of God's presence with humankind in the real world, is communion with God. When God's call to communion is neglected or under-played in significance in the proclamation of the Church and its theology, it has often prompted a spiritual movement such as Methodism in the eighteenth century or the Holiness Movement of the nineteenth century which grew under the influence of Phoebe Palmer (1807–1874).

Fourthly, communion with God is not the realization of God's gracious presence in a single moment of conversion, though occasionally it may well begin with such an experience. Rather, fifthly, disappointing experience of the world means we need regular reminders of the deeper spiritual reality which is the real human world. Worship, prayer, sacramental celebration and encouragement of theological reflection are opportunities to reaffirm that we live in the presence of God.

IV

And in America – Freedom

The doctrine of prevenient grace had a particular relevance for the development of Methodist theology in America where the situation was markedly different from that which pertained in England. For English Methodism, the theological framework was provided by Anglicanism. This was not simply because Wesley respected the tradition which had nurtured him, but because the Established Church had constitutional privileges and legal rights which required other Christian communities to define their position. It took Methodism many years to establish itself as an independent Church: in effect it did so after Wesley's death in 1791.

The Plan of Pacification, agreed by Conference of 1795 author-ized ministers to celebrate the sacraments without Episcopal ordination and in 1836 Conference approved the ordination of ministers by the laying on of hands.

For American Methodists, on the other hand, the situation was quite different: Methodism was introduced to America by lay persons. There was no generally authorized pattern of Christian believing because there existed no ecclesial authority against which Methodism had to define itself or defend itself. Methodism in America is therefore very particularly a Movement. It took its form and sought to find its way as an evangelical body, moving westward with the people, preaching the gospel in response to the circumstances it found. While it honoured Wesley and his vision, he did not have the personal status or theological influence in the American Methodist Church that he enjoyed in England.

Local leaders were dominant through sheer personality, com-mitment and hard work, especially John Asbury who arrived in 1765 having been sent by John Wesley himself and later Thomas Coke who was controversially ordained by Wesley in 1784 to be the Superintendant of the Methodist Church in America. Asbury, a spiritual man and brilliant manager, held together an extensive itinerant body consisting of some 700 preachers by 1812, though according to his contemporary Nathan Bangs (1778–1862), he lacked the talent to preach. Their authority was scripture, and their enterprise, the establishment of the Kingdom of God after the pattern of the Early Church. Theological enquiry in American Methodism has continued to benefit from the sense of freedom inherent in its beginning.

American Methodism became an independent Church after the Baltimore Conference of 1784. It immediately found itself in a theological environment dominated by Calvinism brought to America by persecuted European immigrants. Calvinism was a powerful force because it did not pose the same threat to political authority, as existed in England. It offered an over-arching divine power and a spiritual authority to support it which, in the absence of a 'nation state' with a defined constitution and legal powers, many found comforting. Perhaps much of contemporary American society embraces fundamentalist Christianity because it appears to offer a spiritual defence against what many regard as the overweening power of the state, and a way of life based upon the impersonal authority of science and technology.

Notwithstanding the profound influence of Calvinism, with its belief in the total depravity of humankind, it is apparent that there were those even within Calvinism who held that God had not totally determined the ultimate destination of every human soul. Covenantal Calvinism, for example, sometimes referred to as 'conditional covenant', was very influential in New England. Its theological perspective was not as exclusive as that which existed in England. There was, they believed, a human dimension to salvation which allowed that the human will might have even a necessary place in the divine scheme of things.

Methodism rejected the predestinarianism of Calvin, in America as in Britain. Asa Shinn (1781–1865), has some claim to be the first person within American Methodism to take theology seriously. He asserted that it was impossible to think that the God of the Bible would deprive humankind of the freedom to discern his gracious presence.[8] He thought it the plain meaning of the Bible that grace was offered to every person, a view which implicitly points to the doctrine of prevenient grace. If freedom was the gift of a graciously present omnipotent God then the Church, the community of faith, could preach the gospel with the expectation of being heard.

American Methodists found the Calvinist God narrow, restrictive, too risk-averse and utterly inadequate as an account of God as they experienced him in the freedom of their daily lives. God had authority; that they never denied. But if God was to reveal himself as a God of love, he could not be authoritarian and dictatorial; he would have to be self-disciplined and make himself known in a loving relationship. Christ incarnated God's love in history in such a way as to show that this was the eternal character of all creation, not an accidental phenomenon. The world is so 'graced' that human beings live in an environment in which it is always possible to become aware of God as he is in himself. The Bible witnessed to this as Nathan Bangs averred. 'Christ the true light has come, the Spirit of truth is sent into the world.' At one and the same time three things occurred; awareness of their own sinfulness, awareness of God's presence, a desire to live in the new creation. They willingly acknowledged his authority through becoming obedient to his will: God was indeed authoritative, not authoritarian. Methodist theology in America was liberated to work out its own salvation in fear and trembling, untrammeled by an Established Church and eager to explore the world.

V

The Insidiousness of Sin!

It would be a mistake to suggest that Methodist theology did not take sin seriously. John Wesley certainly did but he was not obsessed by it. He knew from personal experience that struggling against sin in one's own strength was futile and debilitating.

> But though he strive with all his might, he cannot conquer; sin is mightier than he. He would fain escape; but he is so fast in prison, that he cannot get forth. He resolves against sin, but yet sins on: he sees the snare, and abhors and runs into it. So much does his boasted reason avail – only to enhance his guilt, and increase his misery! Such is the freedom of his will; free only to evil; free to 'drink in iniquity like water'; to wander farther and farther from the living God, and do more 'despite to the Spirit of grace.'[9]

But no man is alone: God's prevenient grace means every person is free to choose salvation and will receive the strength to accept God's forgiveness. Wesley knows that only as one gains confidence in the living presence of God can one achieve what in one's best moments one 'naturally' desires with all one's heart – forgiveness and peace of mind in the company of Christ in the presence of God, the Father! The reason is that this transformation is impossible until one recognizes one's sinfulness. One is aware of something taking one where one does not want to go despite all one's best intentions; but because one is ignorant of the deceptive nature of sin, one is obsessed with getting round it, avoiding it, trying to escape it or even just trying to ignore it. But it cannot be done.

In a profound sense, it is prevenient grace – the real presence of God underpinning all existence – that allows us to come to terms with sin. To feel that we are unconditionally accepted by God, as Tillich puts it, means freedom to be honest about our condition and open to personal transformation.[10] The mercy of God is that he only convicts of sin when once we have begun to realize that there is something which we can do about it – when we become aware of prevenient grace.

Wesley's purpose in preaching was to focus minds and hearts on God whose invincible loving presence pre-existed human sin and flourished despite it for the sake of mankind. To be anthropomorphic, one might dare to say that the fact of human sin deepened God's love for man because he identified himself with man's need. The words of the *Exultet* on Holy Saturday ring true:

> O happy fault, which has deserved to have such and so mighty a Redeemer.[11]

Stanley Hauerwas, following Shusaku Endo, talks of 'salvation even in sin: learning to tell the truth about ourselves'. I ask myself whether there can be anything else?[12] Without sin with all its awful associations, there would be no possibility of becoming aware of one's God-given freedom and the deep-rooted human desire to do good and to *be* good. In fact, there would be no chance of salvation.

Our everyday experience provides insight here. Every good teacher knows that the art of teaching is to inspire enjoyment in learning. When once that has been achieved, the pupil will become conscious of his ignorance but know that he can do something about it. All depends on the pupil's awareness of the teacher's commitment to him, and on the recognition that he can learn. The good teacher works to make the pupil an independent learner.

By analogy one might say, that to be a sinner is to relax into a state in which you are content with the assumption that there is nothing that you can do about your condition. To be saved is to realize that you can improve the situation because you understand that you are not alone: God believes in and is committed to you becoming an independent person. You gain the courage to be and are transformed after the image of Christ in full knowledge that, as St Irenaeus wrote, 'the glory of God is man fully alive and the life of man is the vision of God'.[13]

St Paul says we have all fallen short of the glory of God; that is we have failed to recognize God's presence and come to believe that we must try to live as if he did not exist.[14] This is our mistake. The fact is that God is present, which is affirmed and celebrated in the doctrine of prevenient grace. To be human means to share something with the nature of God, to be in God's image. Eastern Orthodoxy talks advisedly of divinization!

VI

Original Sin

But this is surely to underestimate the ingrained nature of sin in humankind. Article VII of the Articles of Religion of the United Methodist Church states:

Original sin standeth not in the following of Adam (as the Pelagians talk), but it is the corruption of the nature of every man, that naturally is engendered of the offspring of Adam, whereby man is very far gone from original righteousness, and of his own nature inclined to evil, and that continually.[15]

The British Methodist Church takes its doctrinal standards from 'the doctrines of the evangelical faith' as 'contained in Wesley's *Notes on the New Testament* and the first four volumes of his sermons'.[16] Sermon XXXVIII is on *Original Sin*. Wesley was persuaded of the reality of original sin and frequently referred to it. He dedicated the longest of his theological writings to the topic.[17] He wrote it to refute John Taylor (1694–1761) who adopted a neo-Pelagian position arguing that original sin was the result of the misuse of human freedom and not as Article IX of the Anglican *Articles of Religion* had it, the consequence of Adam's sinful disobedience. Wesley believed sin to be more than misguided behaviour.

Given the weight of this evidence in the Methodist tradition, it is interesting that in my researches for this book I have found the term 'sin' to be conspicuously under-discussed. Has it any relevance in the contemporary life and teaching of Christianity in general and Methodism in particular? In my opinion it has, but care is necessary in how we approach it, for to misconstrue it is as fatal to human health and salvation as the attempt to ignore it.

Wesley's theology and subsequent Methodist understanding sheered away from any notion of imputed guilt. Methodism has rather tended towards a view of original sin as corruption, thus following the eastern rather than the western tradition. Any imputed guilt if such existed, could be discounted because at birth it was cancelled through God's redemption of the world and all humanity in Christ. Genesis has it that man is made in the image of God.[18] If so, then does the notion of original sin involve the total loss of God's image in man or an in principle modification of the image which while crucial, leaves the possibility of being in the image of God intact? The doctrine of God as Trinity indicates that the primary image of God's nature is 'Being in eternal loving relationship'. This is sensitively and creatively expressed in the eastern tradition of *perichoresis*, – each Person of the Trinity exists in and for the others. This dynamic insight affirms that the psychological truth and divine perspective about personal relationship are one: only in giving oneself to the other is one who one is.

The claim that man is made in God's image implies that man embodies an analogous capacity for personal, affectionate, other-directed life. The doctrine of original sin expresses exactly the contrary experience: the common human sense of lost personal relationship, separation and being abandoned to one's own devices. This sense of loss, according to the account in Genesis, covers relationships with nature, with other people, with oneself and most significantly, since it is the quality of this relationship that underpins the realization of the others, a loss of any sense of relationship with God.

But this sense of loss is based on the profound mistake of believing that God has withdrawn from us. The condition which results from this false belief is what we call original sin, a false sense of being abandoned by God. The freedom to choose life is

God-given and always open to us: God is incapable of destroying God's gift of himself, or denying the potential divinization of man.

In his sermon, *Justification by Faith*,[19] Wesley recognizes the condition of humankind to be the consequence of disobedience to God's will. In paradise all was well, and could have remained so since God had endowed humankind with the ability to enjoy God-given freedom. But through ignorance and misunderstanding of the situation, humankind lost the sense of freedom which came through awareness of a loving relationship with God and sought to manage its own affairs. The consequence was endless repetitive nothingness; without freedom there is no direction, just one thing after another, no opportunity, justice or peace. The dramatic potential of the human condition stopped dead outside the larger world of freedom to be shared with God. The fear of 'the wrath to come' with which one lives on a daily basis in such a world is exactly what one is freed from when one accepts the fact of a loving, eternally present and omnipotent God. Nothing that humankind had done, nothing that any individual human being could do will remove God from God's world.

The liberation of the human spirit into a new and living hope which Wesley offered in his preaching was not magic for in a profound sense the situation had not changed, but it was revolutionary. God was who God was – and is and will be; God, the Creator, Redeemer and eternally present Spirit ached for humankind to do what he was capable of doing, recognize God and engage freely with him in his creative activity. God had revealed himself in Christ as Father, and confirmed humankind as his 'adopted sons'.

VII

The Fatherhood of God in Later Methodist Theology

Methodist theology in North America defined itself in relation to Calvinism, and developed in faith and hope as the circuit riders trekked west with the settlers. In the nineteenth and twentieth centuries the influence of new philosophies, the changing cultural scene and the evolving political situation especially the Civil War and its aftermath, together with the growth of the economy made a powerful impact. Wesley had little direct influence until the revival of interest in his theology in the second half of the twentieth century.

Methodism found itself a 'new' phenomenon in a challenging situation comparable to that of the Early Church. Methodism was free to take charge of its own affairs with a view to the establishment of the Kingdom of God. The vision fitted the ambition entertained by some in American society at large. Indeed, Wilbur Fisk Tillett (1854–1936), a professor of systematic theology at Vanderbilt University talked of the United States as having been established by God with the particular responsibility of bringing in the Kingdom. Missionary activity, Tillett believed, had taken news of the divine redemption of the world through Christ across America and would continue until the whole world had been brought to Christ. This was a task in which Methodism as evidenced by its success had a special place.

The powerful image of God as Father of all was true to American experience and inspired a vision of things to come when all would be included in God's family. Tillett called the first chapter of his first book 'The Fatherhood of God'.[20] It was by taking God's proffered hand and walking with him that through faithful living of the Christian life, salvation would be brought to all. All could enjoy the freedom of membership of God's family in the New World, informed by an Arminian theology. God's prevenient grace implied that God was available to all and underlined the vital importance of preaching the gospel.

In England Wesleyan Methodism stood doctrinally within the Church of England, despite the differences in ecclesiology. John, and most particularly Charles Wesley, felt that despite their commitment to the Methodist societies, they had never left the Church of England. It would be true, I think, to say that English Methodism felt orphaned and abandoned by its family. Perhaps it was this experience which unconsciously stimulated two great British Methodist leaders of the nineteenth and twentieth centuries to think carefully about the Fatherhood of God.

Hugh Price Hughes (1847–1902), hailed from South Wales. He was the son of a Methodist doctor which indicates the change in the social make-up of the Methodist Church which came about during the nineteenth century. He began preaching at the age of 14 and went on to enter the Wesleyan Methodist ministry. He founded *The Methodist Times* which had a major impact on Methodism but his influence extended widely into national life. He embraced the principles of Christian Socialism which was founded by J. M. F. Ludlow (1821–1911) after experiencing the 1848 revolutions when living in Paris. Christians accepted that all were equal in the sight of God, but more needed to be done to ameliorate the awful conditions in which many lived. F. D. Maurice and Charles Kingsley ensured that the Movement was brought to public notice. Hughes spread the ideas in non-conformist circles becoming himself the leading representative of what became known as The Nonconformist Conscience. He saw the need for moral reform in public and private life. He blamed poor housing, shocking working conditions, lack of educational opportunity and the ravages of gambling and drink: he did his best to improve them but realized that progress would require legislation.

He was a remarkable evangelist who established the West London Mission in 1887 where the superintendant minister was later the redoubtable Labour Peer, the Rev'd The Lord Soper (1903–1998). Both Price Hughes and Donald Soper bore witness to the social gospel by which they meant the vision of a society whose business, pleasure and politics in the widest sense were imbued with the love of God in Christ. Hughes' theology was dominated by the vision of God as Father. He regarded theology as speculative and impractical, and rejoiced that it was being replaced by the more human dynamic of biblical scholarship. Careful commentary on the text of scripture and the lively outpouring of the Spirit would inspire the faithful Christian community to establish the Kingdom of God. Theology was practical – to be worked out through worship, political engagement and moral authority. Every Christian who understood faith responsibly could see that each human being was equally valuable to God, and that any circumstance which interfered with the possibility of that realization, was contrary to God's will. To believe in God, as Wesley said, meant both accepting God and doing his will.

Hughes was not a socialist in any real political sense, yet it would be true to say that his vision of God as Father of all, and of all persons as potentially members of the Christian family involved a courtesy and attention to individual need which was not universally recognized at the time.

It is interesting that contemporary research suggests that greater equality in society and between societies could facilitate better social relations and lead to a society with less conflict, more contented and just.[21] While a more equal spread of wealth among a community is implicit in this judgement, equality has implications of a moral, spiritual and personal kind with which Hughes would certainly concur.

John Scott Lidgett (1854–1953) was prompted into action by personal wrestling with a classical problem of theology, the doctrine of the atonement. Wesley could not accept that a loving, just, concerned and omnipotent God would create a divinely determined world. Lidgett did not believe that the Father of Jesus Christ demanded the sacrificial death of his Son in settlement of a debt owed to him for disobedience on the part of the human race. No God of love could stand on the sidelines waiting for his due: it did not make sense.

Moreover, he had the example of his own father whom he admired and with whom he had a fine relationship. Far from being what we today regard as the typical image of a distant and aloof Victorian father, Mr Lidgett Snr. was said by his son to possess a 'radiantly gracious fatherliness'. If Lidgett experienced such affection and concern from his human father, how much more his heavenly Father!

Lidgett was well-educated and widely read. He was familiar with the writings of the German theologians, the politics of Spencer, the evolutionary theory of Charles Darwin, the writings of Cardinal Newman and the social theology of F. D. Maurice and Charles Kingsley. He held them together in a lively tension which he worked out in a theology of social action and in the service of the wider church. In particular he believed that as a devout Wesleyan, he was required to be ecumenical. In the first instance that meant uniting the divergent traditions of British Methodism,

Primitive, United and Wesleyan. He should be regarded as a Catholic Protestant.

The 1881 Conference of British Methodism considered the revision of the catechism. To the question 'What is God?' the existing catechism answered, 'An infinite and eternal spirit'. This had theoretical merit and recommended itself to those of an abstract turn of mind. However, for William Burt Pope (1822–1903), a North American Methodist who had returned to England for his education and remained, becoming a tutor in systematic theology at Didsbury College, Manchester, this failed to represent the experience of the ordinary Methodist. He argued for a more personal approach. The question should be 'Who is God?' and the answer, 'Our Father'. Lidgett was familiar with the debate: discussion with Pope fixed it in his mind.

He like Hugh Pryce Hughes was influenced by F. D. Maurice to work tirelessly both in practice and in theological reflection to hold together life and faith so that an intelligent Christian could get to grips with it and apply it. He wanted a theology faithful to the tradition but enlivened by conversation with contemporary social issues. He wanted to rid Methodism of what he regarded as the outworn philosophical, scientific, legal and moral conceptions inherent in conventional Methodist thinking about God and God's relationship with the world and humankind. His first publication, *The Spiritual Principle of the Atonement*,[22] provides the key to what he developed later in *The Fatherhood of God in Christian Life and Thought*.[23] He affirmed that the love of God revealed in the life and death of Jesus Christ should be understood as 'the grace that bestows' rather than 'the will that ordains', which alludes yet again to prevenient grace (though he did not use the term). Here he believed was the fundamental Christian and therefore Methodist position on the atonement. God's saving work in Christ was achieved through Christ's willing obedience: this it was that revealed the love of his Father. There was nothing slick or compromising about this. The tradition was affirmed, but the meat of it expressed without recourse to the image of a business or legal transaction. The 'cost' to God was the joy of giving himself to his Son's life and work. Christ's pain was God's pain. In his suffering, God expresses his love for all mankind.

Lidgett made this clear when he wrote about the Fatherhood of God. In contradistinction with other strongly held views, Lidgett did not accept that there was some external law to which God had to conform if he was to be just in his relationship with mankind. To talk of God as Father he wrote, 'necessitated our conceiving of the creation of mankind as the calling into existence by God, *out of his own life,* beings at once kindred with Himself and having a distinct individuality of their own'.[24] As the Father of all mankind, which Jesus revealed God to be, God simply was what we might call 'Love in Action', – rather than a God who had to consider what the law was and whether he was willing to see through the costly business of satisfying it. Moreover, Lidgett held together in a dynamic unity God's creating of the world, God's incarnation and redemption, Christ's life and passion and the living presence of the Holy Spirit. This is what led Lidgett to see that the Trinity was at the heart of Christian and therefore of Methodist theology. God, the Creator, identified himself with his Son in his giving of himself for the world's sake, thereby redeeming it and in the eternal work of the Spirit committing himself to seeing the world through to its perfection in relationship with him.

He faced much criticism. On the one hand he was accused of universalism, as if by arguing that God is the Father of All, all could simply assume that they were saved. On the other, he was accused of failing to recognize that the very designation of God as Father somehow involved the notion of eternal punishment because God's fatherly love of all must involve the rejection of those 'sons' who rejected his love. Lidgett's response was to trace his theology to its biblical roots in his last work, a commentary on the Epistle to the Ephesians, and to ground it in the spiritual experience of Methodists. As a true Wesleyan, Lidgett held that faith and practice should be held together in one seamless robe. As Thomas A. Langford says,

> Wesley understood theology to be intimately related to Christian living and the proclamation of Christian faith. Theology is actualized in authentic living and true proclamation. He had little interest in theology for its own sake. Rather, theology was for the purpose of transforming personal life and social relations. This was his 'practical

divinity.' For Wesley, theology was not so much for the purpose of understanding life as for changing life; theology should help effect the love of God and neighbor.[25]

One cannot take this distinction too literally since while Wesley's focus was certainly on human salvation, that depended upon clear thinking about God's nature, his character and manner of relating to human kind. Wesley was not simply a pragmatist; hence, of course, Wesley's Arminianism and rejection of predestination.

In Lidgett's case his acceptance of God as the Father of All led to the foundation of the Bermondsey settlement to serve the poor in one of the toughest areas of London, his co-operation with the Archbishop of Canterbury to establish a chaplaincy service in the British army in the First World War, and above all perhaps his lifelong work in support of education. Education was not of itself the way to salvation, but without a good education a person would be unable to gain the material well-being necessary for a healthy life or to contribute to the common good. He was convinced of Wesley's essential doctrine that all men, however sinful, were called to share God's life in God's family.

VIII

Conclusion

Wesley's vision was of a God who embraced the whole world in his love in order to bring it to the perfection of creaturely sharing in the life of God, Father, Son and Holy Spirit. Methodist theology is focused on engaging with all human experience in the light of this faith so as to share in God's purpose for the world. This certainly means mission in the normal understanding of the term – the bringing of the good news of God's loving presence to every person – but it also means mission in a much wider sense – engaging with all areas of human enquiry and experience so as to grow in theological understanding and faithfulness.

Chapter 6

A World Without Boundaries

Introduction

Methodism knows itself to be part of the Christian Church that is nothing if not 'mission-shaped'. Our vocation in association with the universal Christian community is to partner God in bringing the whole creation to perfection in Christ through the Holy Spirit.

The Church's Commission

The longer ending of St. Mark's Gospel (16.15) reports the occasion when the Risen Christ launched his disciples on the enterprise: 'Go into all the world and proclaim the good news to the whole creation'. Wesley offered 'an intimate, an uninterrupted union with God, a constant enjoyment of Three-in-One God, and of all the creatures in Him'.[1] All creation shares in the potential fulfilment of God's purpose in creation; in the light of this we are called now in the Church to take the living Word of God to the world and to enjoy a quality of life which makes God's salvific presence plain to all.

Methodist missiology finds much to agree with in *Ad Gentes*, the statement of Vatican II on *The Missionary Activity of the Church*.

Sent by God to the nations to be 'the universal sacrament of salvation', the church by the innermost requirements of its own catholicity and in obedience to the command of its founder, strives to proclaim the gospel to all mankind.[2]

> The pilgrim church is of its very nature missionary, since it draws its origin from the mission of the Son and the mission of the Holy Spirit, in accordance with the plan of God the Father.[3]

Methodism's missionary aspiration in all its aspects is grounded in the eternal loving community of the holy Trinity. The purpose of bringing all people to share in the life of God involves a search for the way of truth, service of the vulnerable and strenuous efforts to heal the wounds in the Body of Christ, the One, Holy, Catholic and Apostolic Church. It also sets about a respectful dialogue with those who do not yet accept the gospel believing that we 'can profit from this dialogue by learning to appreciate better those elements of truth and grace which are found among peoples, and which are, as it were, a secret presence of God'.[4] I quote this because it illustrates just how catholic is the vision implicit in Methodist theology.

There is analogy here between the confidence with which the natural world was opened to scientific enquiry, and the world of human history opened up to missionary enterprise. The doctrine of prevenient grace underpins them both. It dawned on us gradually that the world was the creation of God who was affectionate, courteous and attentive. His presence formed the essential quality of the relationships that give life to the world. If God is with us in our enquiring, and in the natural world which we are exploring, who on earth could be against us? Since God enlivens the world with his presence, good scientific enquiry brings us implicitly into relationship with God, not simply with physical events. This is what is affirmed when we refer to the world as creation.

Much earlier in human history, the same doctrine of prevenient grace underpins the Christian approach to the human world. Christ, the Word of God, they realized, has effected the salvation of all people, not just the small gathered communities who met for worship. It was not achieved by the single event of the crucifixion, but in the totality of Jesus' life, teaching, sacrificial death, resurrection and ascension, in which he revealed God to be his father, the Father of all and declared the world to be graced by God's presence.

We are emboldened to take the gospel to the world because the world in all its dimensions, historical and natural, is graced, infused with the loving presence of God. The thankfulness which we express to God through Christ, embraces a love for the natural world and for our fellow human beings which is a necessary condition of accepting our Christian responsibility for the world which is likewise unlimited.

The ambition of Methodist thinking about mission has developed over the course of its history but the vision remains the same. Nothing is excluded from union with Christ, a perception which implies hard theological work in order to show the coherence of our understanding of human experience with the gospel. This is explicit in the important statement on ecclesiology which the British Methodist Conference approved in 1999.

> According to the Bible, the mission of God to the world, that is God's outgoing, all-embracing love for his creation, began with the act of creation itself.
>
> In the death and resurrection of Jesus, Christians saw both the completion of God's mission and the decisive evidence that God reigns – in and through the love which allowed itself to be crucified for the sake of the world.[5]
>
> The unity of the Church and its mission are closely related, since the Triune God who commissions the Church is One, seeking to reconcile and to bring the world itself into a unity in Christ.[6]

Whether it is reasonable to refer to an *act* of creation is a moot point, but one can see the direction of travel: nothing from beginning to end is outside the loving purpose of God.

The United Methodist Church at its General Conference in Forth Worth, Texas, in 2008 'refined the denomination's mission statement to infuse a mission directive into the life and work of the church'. The original statement had stated simply, 'The mission of the Church is to make disciples of Jesus Christ.' Bishop Gregory Palmer, President of the Council of Bishops, reported that the Council of Bishops had asked itself, 'to what end did the church make disciples of Jesus Christ?' The resulting statement now reads, 'The mission of the church is to make disciples of Jesus

Christ for the transformation of the world.' This emphasizes the all-inclusive perspective of discipleship.[7]

The Christian Churches are united in bearing witness to the universal claims of the gospel and the authority of Christ. They flow from the affectionate urgency of St. Matthew who at the close of his gospel reports the women's experience of the glorious drama of resurrection. 'Mary Magdalene and the other Mary' had gone to the tomb to care for Jesus' body only to be taken aback by an earthquake and an angel in white garments descending from heaven. The earthquake and the appearance of an angel in shining white clothing suggest eschatological significance – the beginning of the end, the final revelation. The angel rolled away the stone from the cave in which Jesus was buried and comforted them in their distress.

> 'Do not be afraid,' the angel said, 'I know that you are looking for Jesus who was crucified. He is not here; for he has been raised, as he said. Come see the place where he lay. Then go quickly and tell his disciples, "He has been raised from the dead, and indeed he is going ahead of you to Galilee; there you will see him." This is my message for you.' So they left the tomb quickly with fear and great joy, and ran to tell his disciples. Suddenly Jesus met them and said, 'Greetings!' And they came to him, took hold of his feet, and worshipped him. Then Jesus said to them, 'Do not be afraid; go and tell my brothers to go to Galilee; there they will see me.'
>
> Now the eleven disciples went to Galilee, to the mountain to which Jesus had directed them. When they saw him, they worshipped him; but some doubted. And Jesus came and said to them, 'All authority in heaven and on earth has been given to me. Go therefore and make disciples of all nations, baptizing them in the name of the Father and of the Son and of the Holy Spirit and teaching them to obey everything that I have commanded you. And, remember, I am with you always, to the end of the age.'[8]

The joyous faith of Christians is rooted in the experience of these two women who in effect become the first missionaries. They set off to tell the eleven, as the angel had instructed them, and meet the Risen Christ. All subsequent missionary work is based on this expectation: in taking the good news to others, we meet the Risen Christ. The women are stunned and brought to their knees, but Jesus tells them they have things to do. 'Do not be afraid; go and tell my brothers to go to Galilee; there will they see me'.

His brothers are the Eleven, the disciples whom Jesus had tried to introduce into his conversation with God. But they misunderstood and believed that their hopes were dashed by the crucifixion. Their false hopes were dashed: Jesus did not promise power, riches or influence in any material sense. But Jesus' hope was not destroyed because his hope was based on trust in his relationship with God, his Father. When they had asked him to teach them how to pray, he had taught them to call God 'Father'. They should join with him in his prayer, and pray '*Our Father*' but this at the time was too ordinary for them; it sounded like *'Daddy'*.

But they did go to Galilee and there met Jesus. Matthew has Jesus speaking in a very matter of fact manner. 'All authority' he says, 'has been given to me in heaven and in earth'. And he commissions them to preach and make disciples of all nations. Perhaps they are beginning to understand something of what God has done in Jesus and that there are consequences, responsibilities, privileges, doubts and joys that will be theirs forever. But at the same time they grasp that there is nothing to fear for, whatever happens, Jesus will be with them always; and, so therefore will God their Father. Jesus' words, 'And, remember, I am with you always,' close the gospel and begin a new world. Perhaps they can really pray with Jesus, 'Our Father'! It is not possible to say that the reference to baptizing in the name of the Father and of the Son and of the Holy Spirit represents a fully developed Trinitarian doctrine, since there is no evidence to support such a claim elsewhere in the New Testament. But nevertheless, the language is in the gospel on which future generations could draw.

Jesus' commission of the disciples informed John Wesley's vision: attention to it helps us to gain perspective on his theology as he entered into the tradition of the Christian faith and accepted the responsibilities flowing from being Christ's brother and fellow worker. His approach to the Church, to the gospel, to mission, to preaching, recapitulates what he believed to be the situation in the

Early Church. His study of the Bible and of the Church Fathers allows him to tell the story of the gospel to himself all over again. The first disciples had at this point begun to grasp, however dimly, that all power had been given to Jesus whose familiarity with God was such that God dwelt in him and he in God; there could be no fear therefore of anything that might befall anyone in Christ. And John Wesley, like those first disciples, felt that freedom from fear for himself. No one in the world, past, present or future should be deprived of the opportunity to know God in Christ for them-selves. They could and would hear the gospel, if John Wesley had his way and was obedient to the heavenly vision.

Charles Wesley, too, was caught up in the same vision and taught Methodists to sing heartily in glorious, confident song. The sense of grateful optimism permeates many of his hymns.

> Power is all to Jesus given,
> Lord of hell, and earth, and heaven,
> Every knee to him shall bow;
> Satan, hear, and tremble now.[9]

> Nature is subject to thy word,
> All power to thee is given,
> The uncontrolled, almighty Lord
> Of hell, and earth and heaven.[10]

> See on the mountain top
> The standard of your God!
> In Jesu's name I lift it up,
> All stained with hallowed blood.

> His standard-bearer I
> To all the nations call:
> Let all to Jesu's cross draw nigh!
> He bore the cross for all.[11]

> Come, Father, Son, and Holy Ghost,
> Honour the means ordained by thee!
> Make good our apostolic boast,
> And own thy glorious ministry.

We now thy promised presence claim,
Sent to disciple all mankind,
Sent to baptize into thy name,
We now thy promised presence find.[12]

Charles celebrates the authority, power and presence of Christ here in their manifestation of God's glory. There was nothing to limit the claims implicitly made here for the Risen Christ: how could there be because the claims were rooted in Charles' understanding of God. Heaven, hell, nature, sin and all the powers of evil were under his feet: nothing had power over the God and Father of our Lord, Jesus Christ. God was redemptively creative, available for all, irremovably present with and in his Creation, absolutely committed to its perfection, powerful in the dynamic vigour of his Holy Spirit. When once one has grasped the sense of what John and Charles Wesley had glimpsed of the free grace of God alive in Christ, conversation is possible with everyone, every philosophy, every discipline of enquiry, all religions and novel ideas, with a view to extending the range of the authority of the Kingdom of God.

For Wesley and Methodists subsequently, the intellectual and moral justification for mission was grounded in God and the realization of his presence. However, a great deal of intelligent enquiry, conversation, prayer and reflection is necessary if the significance is to be unpacked and acted upon. Hence the aspects of the relationship between God, Father, Son and Holy Spirit expressed or implicit in the last chapter of St. Matthew are very important and revealing. God in Jesus Christ goes before his disciples; they are embraced as his brothers, and driven in his presence to prayer and worship. They are commissioned to preach, teach, baptize all nations into their fellowship and assist them to celebrate God's presence in worship; above all Christ is with them in every situation and for all time.

But if they are to know this for themselves and feel themselves to be sharing in God's work – the *Missio Dei* – they will have to take risks and venture trustingly into the unknown world where they are likely to meet opposition, conflict, misunderstanding and even persecution. Only in obedience to his life-giving command will they the 'promised presence find'. This seems to me to be the key to understanding the motivation, ambition and enterprise of the Methodist Movement from its beginning. One can sense the excitement as well as the daunting nature of the responsibility which Methodists felt and, it is to be hoped, still feel.

Of course, the Church catholic and every Christian denomination makes universal claims. The contrasting theological positions of the Roman Catholic Church and Orthodoxy naturally embody this since they trace their history from the very beginnings of the faith. Other traditions, Lutheran, Calvinist, Baptist, Congregational, Presbyterian and Anglican, for example, also claim a worldwide mission. But while they too claim to be rooted in the origins of Christianity they stem from specific points of doctrinal disagreement and in the case of Anglicanism find root also in political dispute. Methodism claims a worldwide mission which is differently based since there is no essential intent to diverge from the Catholic Faith; rather it is focused upon bearing witness to it among people whom they believe need to be reminded of it or who have been denied the opportunity to hear the gospel. The poor, the outcast, the neglected and all who live in parts of the world not yet aware of the freedom that comes from knowing Christ.

Moreover, a theology which suggests that God has limited his gift of himself to a small number is alien to the gospel and must be opposed. The gospel is for all. No more than God himself, does the Church have the power to force belief in Christ on the nations of the world; indeed the result of the use of forceful persuasion of any kind is counterproductive. Albert Bledsoe (1809–1877), a Methodist university teacher and opponent of Calvinism was quite clear, morality cannot be compelled even by God – and if not morality, then certainly not faith; both are dependent upon the exercise of freewill.

III

A Movement without Boundaries: A Conversation without Limits

Methodist theology is rooted in the culture of the eighteenth-century evangelical revival which arose alongside the intellectual world of the Enlightenment. It sensed a liberty of thought based on scripture, consistent with tradition and grounded in the celebration of God's presence, which equipped it to engage without fear with the whole world of human experience. There is no limit to its engagement with the world, local, national or international.

God's raising of Jesus convinced John Wesley of the universal presence of the Risen Christ. As the Body of Christ the Church could accept no limit to its gospel ministry; as a minister of the gospel, neither could John Wesley. It is natural therefore that Methodism should think of itself as a movement without boundaries, free to debate with whomsoever and able to infiltrate anywhere. The first limit to be challenged on ecclesio-theological grounds was the parish. Methodism in Britain emerged only gradually from Anglicanism and indeed its theology continues to be essentially Anglican. However, when Wesley was prevented from preaching by an unsympathetic Episcopal authority as concerned for public order as the gospel, he took the law into his own hands as we have seen. God's grace was freely available for all and so neither legal threat nor public violence should be allowed to frustrate the Word of God.

Wesley undoubtedly regretted quarrelling with bishops but he believed it his calling to bear witness to the Christ wherever he was, whatever the circumstances. Moreover, was there not evidence that God blessed his work? Thousands came to Christ through open air preaching who would not otherwise have heard the gospel. He wrote in his Journal on 11 June 1739,

> I look upon all the world as my parish; thus far I mean,
> that, in whatever part of it I am, I judge it meet, right, and
> my bounden duty to declare unto all that are willing to
> hear, the glad tidings of salvation. This is the work which
> I know God has called me to; and sure I am that his
> blessing attends it.

The implications of this for Methodist theology have been profound, though rather different in the two primary foci of Methodism, North America and Britain.

British Methodism worked within the constraint of the Established Church; it was by many regarded as an outsider, an intruder which, however well-meaning and successful, threatened the decent conventions of public religious life. The denomination was held together as it expanded by Wesley's force of personality, organizational skill and preaching. It did not reject the Episcopal office in principle but placed it in the annual Conference and the circuit superintendant minister. Many attempts have been made to reunite with the Church of England; all have so far failed. But the continued coherence of Anglican and Methodist doctrine has led British Methodist theological scholars to make their contribution to theological enquiry through biblical scholarship and historical studies rather than systematic or philosophical theology.[13]

In North America, on the other hand, in the absence of an established church preachers were unconstrained by parish boundaries and free to embrace an Episcopal system. The Baltimore Conference of 1784 declared Methodism to be Episcopal, and replaced the title 'superintendant' with 'Bishop' in 1787. This marked the creation of an independent American Methodist Church. Itinerancy was affirmed because it suited particularly well the mobile and growing American population.

The consequence for theology in America has been far greater freedom and encouragement for Methodists to think through theological ideas in the varied situations in which they found themselves and with the influences which impacted upon them. Immigrants from continental Europe, especially Germany and Scandinavia, brought their theological education and ecclesiological traditions with them. Their more philosophical, cultural and political education profoundly influenced Methodist theological thinking and tended to encourage scholars to study in Germany rather than in England. But in every context the style of Methodist thinking has been influenced by conversation rather than confrontation, conferencing rather than introspection.

The challenge to the boundary of the parish is but one example. The boundary of the state, secondly, was taken to be irrelevant. Britain was part of an expanding world brought about by its burgeoning imperial ambition. Lay Methodists involved in trade and the military took opportunities to establish local societies. American Methodism combined pastoral concern with missionary ambition as it made itself at home in the vast continent and then looked beyond to the wider world.

The world perspective of Methodist preachers, thirdly, challenged cultural barriers as Methodism established itself in Africa, the West Indies and Sierra Leone. Evangelism was concerned to bring people to Christ but important though this was, engaging with other traditions required intelligent conversation if understanding was to grow. This has become much more significant as immigration into Britain post-World War II brought 'world religions' into the homeland. Judaism had been in Britain since the Middle Ages, but significant numbers of Muslims, Hindus and Buddhists have changed the face of Britain and posed interesting questions for the churches with which Methodism swiftly engaged.

IV

Methodism in Ireland: An Example of Missionary Enterprise

Ireland provides an interesting case in point. It demonstrates the practical outworking of a theological position, and willingness to learn from it.

Wesley visited Ireland on some twenty-one occasions at the request of Methodists who had moved to Dublin from England. The religious context was largely Roman Catholic. His first focus was on 'slumbering' Protestants who numbered about 25,000 out of a population of approximately two million, but some Roman Catholics were attracted by his preaching. His attitude to Roman Catholicism was of course traditionally English: he regarded the Pope as a foreign agent, who constituted a threat to the English state and to the Church of England. However, in Ireland he met individual believing Catholics which he hardly had the opportunity for in England where the Roman Catholic Church was not tolerated.

The experience stimulated Wesley to write an open letter dated 18 July 1749, presumably to a lay Catholic, which was published in Dublin in the same year.[14] It is a remarkable testimony to Wesley's 'catholic spirit' and his willingness to test the boundaries in the light of his experience. He refers to the mutual misunderstanding between Catholics and Protestants which he accepts leads to malice, anger and every sort of 'unkind affection'. He thinks there is another way based upon courteous attention for one another in the light of faith in Christ.

> I do not suppose that all bitterness is on your side. I know there is too much on our side too. So much that I fear many Protestants (so-called) will be angry at me, too, for writing to you in this manner and will say, "'Tis showing you too much favour; you deserve no such treatment at our hands.'
>
> But I think you do. I think you deserve the tenderest regard I can show; were it only because the same God hath raised you and me from the dust of the earth and has made us both capable of loving and enjoying him to eternity; were it only because the Son of God has brought you and me with his own blood. How much more, if you are a person fearing God (as without question many of you are) and studying to have a conscience void of offence towards God and towards man.[15]

He explains his Protestant faith and urges that they may love alike even if they cannot yet think alike in all things.

> Let us count all things but loss for the excellency of the knowledge of Jesus Christ our Lord, being ready for him to suffer the loss of all things and counting them but dung, that we may win Christ.

Notwithstanding the unpromising environment, by Wesley's death in 1791 there were six districts, 29 circuits and over 15,000 members in Ireland.

The openness of Irish Methodism had, given its size, a disproportionate influence on the Church. Philip Embury (1728–1775) heard Wesley preach in 1752 and later in 1766 with his cousin, Barbara Heck (1734–1804) emigrated with other unemployed linen workers to New York to seek employment. He was the first Methodist preacher to settle in America; he founded a Methodist society and eventually built a church. Canadian Methodism was served by 200 Irish ministers during the nineteenth century and it was an Irish minister, James Lynch who led the first missionary expedition to Asia, landing in Sri Lanka (Ceylon) in 1813.

The Conference of the Methodist Church in Ireland covers the whole island of Ireland. Commitment to education and reconciliation are key perspectives of the Church's mission. Edgehill College, now a constituent college of Ulster University trains clergy and lay workers and provides courses in theology for the whole island. Consistent with the Methodist ethos which seeks to be 'the friend of all and enemy of none', Edgehill was the first Theological College in Ireland to offer courses where both the teachers and the students are drawn from Catholic and Protestant traditions. The courses are offered in association with the Roman Catholic Mater Dei College of Education. There are two excellent secondary schools, Wesley College Dublin, established in 1845,[16] and Methodist College Belfast, founded in 1865 and several primary schools. The commitment continues: in 1948 Gurteen College, was founded to serve the needs of the rural community in The Irish Republic.

The Church has had a vital role in the peace process consequent upon the Troubles which plagued Northern Ireland from 1969 until the Good Friday Agreement of 2002. Its compassionate history and perhaps even its comparatively small membership, meant that neither side in the conflict regarded it as a threat and it was free to take initiatives. The Rev'd Dr. Eric Gallagher, (1912–2000), a former President of the Methodist Church in Ireland, was in 1974 one of a group of Protestant ministers to meet with IRA and Sinn Fein representatives at Feakle in an abortive attempt to broker a deal. He continued to work for peace in association with Cardinal Cahal Daly (1917–2009) who was himself bravely critical of the IRA. In his address at Dr. Gallagher's funeral, Cardinal Cahil spoke warmly of his contribution.

> Not many people have been clear and steady beacons of light in the darkness of the last thirty years. Eric Gallagher was one. It was a pleasure to work with him . . . he took risks for peace.

The Revd. Harold Good was one of those appointed to verify the Decommissioning of Weapons in 2005.

The powerful witness was not confined to official Church representatives. Gordon Wilson (1927–1995) with his daughter, Marie, attended the Remembrance Day Service at Enniskillin in 1987 which was attacked by bombers. He reported the last conversation he had with his daughter as she lay dying in the rubble. He, only hours afterwards, spoke movingly of his forgiveness of the bombers, promising to pray for them. He urged no reprisals and spent the rest of his life working for reconciliation. The Irish Government honoured him by making him a Senator in the Irish Parliament.

Interestingly, the Methodist Church in Ireland, against the trend for the Christian Church as a whole, has increased in membership (now some 50,000) though it would be impossible to say that the role of Methodism in the Peace Process was the cause. However, the involvement of the Church in Irish public life is consistent with an approach to mission considered as 'the commitment of the Church to the world in God's name for Christ's sake'. The work is risky; it is undertaken without prejudice and in hope, in full confidence that God's prevenient grace underpins all that is worthwhile.

It can justly be said that Wesley's frequent visits to Ireland and his, if not always apparent, courteous attitude to Catholics is still alive and well among the Irish Methodist community: it expresses a general affection towards 'the other' to be 'friends of all and enemies of none'. Irish Methodism's collective focus on the peaceful resolution of conflict was born of confidence built up over many years of ecumenical commitment. It was a founder member of the Irish Council of Churches in 1922, one of the very earliest of National Councils of Churches, and of the Irish Church Meeting founded in 1973 which includes the Roman Catholic Church. This is more than recognition born of practical expediency, it represents a deep theological feeling for the way of truth.

Latterly ecumenical concern has included Inter-Faith questions. A Jewish community has existed in Ireland for centuries but communities of Muslims, Hindus and Buddhists are now growing. Methodism is involved with both the Inter-Faith Forum established in 1993 in Northern Ireland and the Three Faiths Forum inaugurated in Dublin in 1996. A report to the Irish Conference in 2007 concludes with the sentence:

> It is our hope that, inspired by both the great Commission and great Commandment, and drawing on our particular history and experience, the Methodist Church in Ireland, despite its relatively small membership, will give an inter-faith lead in Ireland, based on a firm but generous Wesleyan faith, similar to the lead in ecumenical relations given by Methodist people both in Ireland and in other parts of the world.

Methodism in Ireland is a crucial example of how Methodist theology refuses to accept limits. There is an inherent assumption in Wesleyan theology that no barriers exist, since God in Christ has overcome all divisions and rendered all distinctions void.

V

British Methodism – A Witness to the Risen Christ throughout the World

As a cameo of the way the Methodist Church works out its theology in practice, the case of Irish Methodism is striking. It nourishes the faith of members; in life and worship it celebrates God's presence with his people, recommends the gospel to neigh-bours and the wider world community, and in open conversation with other Christian traditions and other religions looks to estab-lish peace and understanding. Methodism has the same attitude in every place; the consequence is that Methodism is a lively pres-ence within the universal Church.

The British Methodist Missionary Society was founded as a national body in 1818, and over the course of the next century established work in the West Indies, Canada, Africa (East, West and South), the Pacific, India and China. The work was risky: many missionaries for West Africa died within a very short time of their arrival: the passion for the gospel is apparent from the fact that these fatalities did not discourage further volunteers for the mission field.[17] The importance of missionary work had, however, already dawned upon Methodism as the examples of the West Indies and Sri Lanka indicate.

Thomas Coke, the Father of Methodist Missions and widely believed to have been Wesley's preferred successor, was more committed to spreading the gospel 'among the heathens' than to holding high office – though he was secretary to the Conference and twice became President. He published a significant pamphlet on the implications of the gospel for mission in 1783.[18] Wesley did not approve; having failed to get the Bishop of London to consecrate a bishop for America, he saw the more immediate task as support for the societies in America and sent Thomas Coke (1747–1814) as Superintendant in 1784. When Coke returned in 1785 he produced a second pamphlet in 1786 urging mission to the islands around Britain, to Canada, Newfoundland, Quebec, Nova Scotia and the West Indies. He won support and the same year set sail for Newfoundland. However, storms forced him south to Antigua where to his astonishment he found there was already a Methodist society consisting largely of black members. A planter had heard Wesley preach when visiting London, and on his return preached to and won converts among his slaves. The work was extended through the Caribbean when the 1803 British Conference resolved to send missionaries. The critical dimension of slavery was tackled; Thomas Coke had spoken against it in 1785 when in America for the first time. It came to an end finally in British territories with the Act of Emancipation in 1834 which was read by Methodist preachers in their churches throughout the islands.

Thomas Coke's energy and vision were inexhaustible. He had already visited Gibraltar in 1803, visited Sierra Leone and supported missions in Canada and Scotland, but was determined to extend the work to include the East Indies, India and Ceylon (Sri Lanka). Conference initially opposed him, not on theological grounds but out of concern for the cost and for his age. The Irish Conference supported the initiative in 1813: three men were committed out of the many who volunteered including James Lynch most of whose family was Roman Catholic. They sailed in 1813 but Coke died at sea so that it was the Irishman James Lynch who had the distinction of being the first Methodist missionary in Asia when he landed in Sri Lanka.

Methodism is the largest Protestant denomination in Sri Lanka but still exiguous. Missionary concern led the Church to establish homes for the elderly, day-care centres, a hospital and pre-school education. The 32,000 or so members are 45 per cent Tamil, and 55 per cent Sinhalese which gives it a strong position to contribute to peace through education and conflict resolution. Early contacts between Buddhism and Christianity dating from the sixteenth century were hostile. David de Silva, a member of a distinguished Methodist family, worked hard to build mutual respect which led in 1951 to the establishment of the Ecumenical Institute for Society and Dialogue, a major centre for Christian-Buddhist relations. The first two directors were Methodist ministers, the Revd. G. B. Jackson and Lyn de Silva. The Institute continues to grow in influence and is now organized into three Divisions, Centre for Buddhist Studies, Division of Frontier Studies and Division of Studies of Other Faiths.

Following the end of the Second World War as British colonies gained independence, local Methodist Churches which had hitherto been under the direction of the Missionary Society in London also became independent. Methodist churches in the West Indies became the Methodist Church of the West Indies and the Americas in 1967, maintaining close links with British Methodism and also the United Methodist Church of America. Methodism in Sri Lanka became independent in 1964. In both cases, as with other Methodist churches, there has been a strong commitment to continued evangelism, an ecumenical involvement, support for education, health and the poor. Often the earlier major investment in schools, hospitals etc. has been taken over by the state, but the service of the community, the building of relationships across communities and across religious divides has been a distinctive expression of Methodist theology.

VI

The American Missionary Perspective

The Methodist Church in America was itself a missionary enterprise from its very beginning. Itinerant preachers followed the settlers in their movement west and began to work among Native Americans.

The Church split several ways in the course of the nineteenth century for racial and sociological reasons rather than doctrinal. The Evangelical Awakening of the mid-eighteenth century coincided with a shift in moral perspectives which included the anti-slavery movement. There had been protests against slavery by some Roman Catholics but without much impact; Methodist preachers however spoke directly to Africans in West Africa, the West Indies and in America in language which gave them a sense of self-worth. But not all was sweetness and light: a strong body of opinion wanted to separate conversion from freedom. The African Methodist Episcopal Church (AMEC) was a reaction to this. It began in Philadelphia in 1800 when Richard Allen, resentful of the treatment of African-Americans even by some within Methodism, established an independent church. The primary purpose was evangelism, but this could not be separated from the search for social justice. The AMEC began missionary work in Africa in 1820 and now has conferences in Sierra Leone, Liberia, Ghana, Nigeria and the Ivory Coast.

The United Methodist Church inherited the work of its uniting churches who were involved in the agreement of 1939 and 1968. It has since vigorously pursued missionary work which is organized within the existing central authority of the Church, the General Conference which meets every four years. This body speaks for the Church and is exclusively responsible for determining policy. The Jurisdictional or General Conferences are regional meetings accountable to the General Conference which also meet every four years. There are five jurisdictions in the States and seven overseas; namely Africa, Central and Southern Europe, Congo, Germany, Northern Europe, Philippines and West Africa. German, Swiss and Scandinavian immigrants who went to America in the eighteenth and nineteenth centuries formed pietistic communities such as the United Brethren in Christ which were characterized by emphases on personal experience and ecumenical concern. Methodism in continental Europe can largely be traced to emigrants returning home.

Methodism in South America emerged from the middle of the nineteenth century almost accidentally as the result of economic enterprise by British and American firms and military action. There was strong resistance from the Catholic episcopate, but more liberal political and economic developments gradually provided a more encouraging environment for the evangelical churches, Baptist, Presbyterian and Methodist. The establishment in 1969 of The Council of Evangelical Methodist Churches in South America and the Caribbean (CIEMAL) consisting of 19 South American Churches and the Methodist Church in the West Indies, and the recognition of their independence gave a fillip to development. CIEMAL produced a book of worship reflecting local spontaneity and a shared culture with other Protestant churches. Out of the experience of poverty there emerged the dynamic of liberation theology, particularly through the work of the Methodist theologian, José Miguez Bonino (b.1924).

VII

The World Methodist Council

Sharing the experience of others is an inescapable aspect of the Methodist ethos. Hence Methodists meet together in Conference, locally, regionally, nationally and now internationally. Thirty Methodist bodies met in 1881 in Wesley's Chapel, London in an Ecumenical Methodist Conference; only fourteen years after the first Lambeth Conference of the Anglican Church. It changed its name to the World Methodist Council (WMC) in 1951 and established a Headquarters at Lake Junaluska in North Carolina. The Council represents 75 million Methodists from 76 member churches in 132 countries; as a consultative body it has no jurisdiction over the individual member churches though it is gaining influence through the range of its interests. A conference of 500 delegates representing all the member churches meets quinquennially. The need to tackle major economic, social, religious, political and environmental issues from a global perspective will almost certainly add to its authority as the importance of contributing its distinctive voice to the conversation towards human well-being becomes ever more apparent.

The eight standing committees of the WMC indicate the wholeness of the Methodist understanding of mission. They cover

Ecumenical dialogue, education, family life, theological education, evangelism, social and international affairs, worship and liturgy and youth affairs.

The World Methodist Evangelism Institute, established by the Council in 1981 and based at the Candler School of Theology in Emery University, Atlanta represents the contemporary Methodist desire to recover its essential character as a Movement intent upon bringing the world to Christ. This is important: Methodism in the West settled into a comfortable urban environment: mission was associated with work 'overseas'. But the Methodist Missionary Society of the British Methodist Church is the British Methodist Church organized for mission: there is no independent society for missions. That seems right, if one is truly to understand the nature of the Church in all its aspects as the Body of Christ.

VIII

Conclusion

Methodism is practical theology in the sense that it draws life from the living God on whom its attention is focused. The vision of God which it glimpses is in process of becoming clearer and stimulating new ventures in thought and action. Education, health, employment, social justice, politics, care of the world's resources, the spiritual life, deeper understanding of other religions; these and many other commitments are aspects of mission as intuited in Methodist theology. They embody what it means to be in conversation with God in Christ, to have faith in him and to offer him praise and thanksgiving. The commission of the Church is to enter more and more into the mind of Christ so as more effectively to work with God for the fulfilment of his purpose in creation.

Chapter 7

The Mind of Christ

I

Introduction

Conventional wisdom recognizes the importance of early intervention in securing sound human development, whether physical fitness,
intellectual understanding, spiritual maturity or managing disability.
My school experience illustrates this. A. S. Gregory converted to
Roman Catholicism in the 1930s having formerly been a Methodist
minister. It was he who introduced me to Thomist philosophy when
I was a pupil at Kingswood School, Wesley's foundation in Bath.
Thomism made a great impression on me because it re-enforced my
growing feeling that if one was to learn the truth about anything, it
would be consistent with everything else one knew, – or thought
one knew. At the time I was also increasingly intrigued by the questions raised by science for religious belief so I found Professor Charles
A. Coulson's lecture to us in the same series equally stimulating. He
was quite clear that 'either God is in the whole of nature, with no
gaps, or He is not there at all'. These good experiences came to mind
as I thought about this chapter. The conversation which God began
with the world in creation is continuous with the conversation
which Christ took up with his Father and which the Church now
continues: it is dynamic and inclusive. Our missionary task is to
engage with all human experience in order to point to the presence
of God. It is what we call entering into the mind of Christ.

II

The Mind of Christ

Methodist theology participates in the conversation of God with
his world, focused on scripture, developed in tradition, examined

by reason and tested in experience. John Wesley intended in his preaching of the gospel to point to God and the salvation which he offered in Christ to the whole world. The statement of the British Methodist Church already alluded to makes this quite explicit: God gives himself to his creation.

> According to the Bible, the mission of God to the world,
> that is God's outgoing, all-embracing love for his creation,
> began with the act of creation itself.[1]

In order to share God's mission to the world, Methodist theology engages with both God and his creation so as to enter, as much as humanly possible, into the mind of Christ and to do his will.[2] This tells us why Methodism's approach to mission includes more than the important business of making disciples. Bringing the world to Christ is at the heart of the practice of the Faith, but 'the world' is far larger than the persons who inhabit it. Saving souls includes a politico-socio-economic dimension informed by research into our relation with the natural world. Methodism does not, indeed cannot hold apart theology and ethics: love of God and love of neighbour constitute a seamless activity which must include love of God's world in all its dimensions.[3] Fashionable discussion assumes the irrelevance of theology to public life. Our theology assumes the opposite; conversation with theology is integral to debate about both political economy and scientific enquiry. Of course this does not mean that Christians, let alone Methodists are the only people who have sound views on truth and moral questions: Methodists are in no position to say, 'God says . . . .' But it does imply that insights into the personal nature of God in Trinity need to be brought to bear in any discussion of moral questions if a critical dimension of human experience is not to be lost with serious diminishment of our sense of what it is to be human.[4]

Loving God is not a private spiritual relationship with the divine, because to be human is to be a person-in-relation. Moreover, I am not the only influence which bears on my sense of selfhood. For example, my understanding of myself is shaped by the society in which I live and by the nature of the physical world of which I am a part. These facts indicate the extent of the missionary task implicit in loving the world – attending to the well-being of God's creation: God's missionary purpose is cosmic.

First, in the light of God's promise of peace and justice we are called to transform the political and economic relationships between nations, races, genders and generations. We can, if we want, change them to take more account of the fact that humankind is one interdependent community in one world. We are called, in theological language, to realize the Kingdom of God.

Secondly, since we believe the world is created through the Word, we confidently enquire into its nature so that all humanity can live in active harmony with it. The physical world is not over against us to be controlled, but something to be understood and co-operated with. We are called, in theological language, to renew creation.

To take responsibility with God for the world implies that we listen to scientists and technologists, historians, economists and social scientists so that we enhance our capacity to care for creation and offer a better life to all people. It also means that we open ourselves to the stimulus which flows from artists and writers.

This raises the intriguing theological question of the relationship between theology and other disciplines of human enquiry. But of one thing we can be sure: the missionary task of personal evangelism, the transformation of socio-politico-economic relationships and our understanding of the natural world is one coherent calling to enter into the mind of Christ and to do his will. It is to seek and practise 'shalom'. The encouraging feature of Methodist theology is that we believe we are working with God to reveal his presence, not working against the grain.

III

'To all Creation' (Mk.16.15b)

There is a cosmic dimension to Methodist thinking about society; the natural world, and the socio-political-economic situation. We take our sense of personal relationships from our understanding of God as persons–in–relation in Trinity. The Trinity, paradoxical as it may appear, points to the unity of God, to God's holding of all

things together in himself. The *Missio Dei,* in which all Christians
share, testifies to the wholeness of things and to the fact that all
things can work together for good. But the theological questions
which arise are formidable. What does the life, teaching, death,
resurrection and ascension of Jesus Christ have to say to our
human society given our increasing understanding of the natural
world?

St John in his gospel sets the life and work of Jesus, the Word,
in a cosmological perspective which recalls the opening of
Genesis. The evangelist begins here because he wants to do justice
to the significance and authority of Jesus, the Christ. St John even
talks of all things being made through the Word.

> In the beginning was the Word, and the Word was with
> God, and the Word was God. He was in the beginning
> with God. All things came into being through him, and
> without him not one thing came into being. What has
> come into being in him was life, and the life was the light
> of all people. The light shines in the darkness, and the
> darkness did not overcome it.[5]

What does this mean? How can the world be said to be made
through the Word; that is – through Christ. On our answer there
depends the justification for the Church's understanding of the
range of its engagement with the *mission dei.*

St John has a distinctively theological way of putting things.
But while the synoptic gospels have a less obvious cosmic Christology, careful attention reveals that there is no aspect of creation
which is excluded from God's redeeming work. Jesus is concerned
for the health of persons and communities, none is excluded.
The writers employ dramatic ways of claiming God's authority
for Jesus, the demoniac (Lk. 4.31–7), the deaf and dumb (Mk. 7.
31–7) and even or perhaps especially the dead (Mk. 5.22–4, 35–43;
Lk. 8.41–2, 49–56) are all included. Human beings may be of
more worth than sparrows, but not even sparrows are worthless
(Matt. 10. 29–31). God's authority holds sway over everything,
life and death, the wind and the waves. Everything is within the
purview of the cosmic salvation which God offers. When he talks
of the world being made through the Word, St John affirms the

quality of God's self-giving in creation: the sacrifice of Christ is the earnest of his gift of himself.

St Paul takes up Jesus' striking challenge to the world order in his attack on the political, economic and social corruption which he sees around him: the Christian, he says, must accept responsibility for himself and for all humankind. If it is understood correctly, what is required for the world to live in peace and joy is that it recognizes the presence of God. But it fears to believe and struggles against those who witness it.

Human relationships are dependent on the search for justice in the way we treat one another *and* the natural world. So, when Jesus reportedly says in the longer ending of St Mark's Gospel, 'Go into all the world and proclaim the good news to the whole creation,' we should pay special attention to the phrase 'the whole creation'.

'To the whole creation' has usually been understood to be limited to 'all people'. Tyndale's translation is 'to all creatures'; the Authorized Version with which Wesley would have been most familiar, closely follows it, translating the Greek 'to every creature'. However, the Jerusalem Bible, the New English Bible, Ronald Knox, the New Revised Standard Version and the New International Bible say 'to all creation'. This seems truer to Jesus' attitude to God's creation. Gingrich and Arndt, however, specifically limit the meaning of the Greek word *ktisis* (creation) to humankind.[6] This dubious generalization is based on slim evidence especially when one recalls that the longer ending of Mark (16. 9–20) represents a later addition and possibly reflects a more thoughtful theological perception. And anyway Gingrich and Arndt admit the word can mean, 'everything that is created' as it does for St. Paul.

> We know that the whole creation has been groaning in
> labour pains until now; and not only the creation, but we
> ourselves, who have the first fruits of the Spirit, groan
> inwardly while we wait for adoption, the redemption of
> our bodies.[7]

It seems clear that here, by 'creation' St. Paul means 'the universe' and most commentators agree, pointing by way of background to the Old Testament vision of a new heaven and a new earth (Is. 65.17; 66.22). If we are right we glimpse here a very contemporary vision of a complex universe in process of being made by God, enlivened by the Spirit, informed by the mind of Christ, which all humankind is invited to share in bringing to perfection.

Christ opens new worlds for Christian missionary enterprise. The task is to relate everything that pertains to our humanity, personal, societal and natural to the Risen Christ and to act with that faith.

IV

The Mind of Christ: Politics, Economics and Political Economy

These are contentious matters. There is in the West a move to privatize religious faith and to deny religion any role in public life. Alastair Campbell, Director of Communications and Strategy to former UK Prime Minister Tony Blair, famously interrupted a journalist who asked the PM about his Christian Faith with the remark, 'I'm sorry, we don't do God.' The strident preaching of millenarianism and the impact of fundamentalist Islam is making some Americans wary of the influence of religion in public affairs. The Methodist position could not be in greater contrast. For Methodists, theology underpins all moral endeavour. Hence, like Aquinas, John Wesley and later Methodists have associated salvation with happiness, happiness with the virtues and the virtues with wisdom.

To be missionary in one's attitude to the world is not to succumb to the belief that one is bringing something into the world from outside. On the contrary, to be a genuine missionary is to bear witness to the truth, which is that God is present in his world working to bring it to perfection. To know Christ is to be at home in the world: to have the mind of Christ is to know one is at home in God's world. One is called to work out what it means to be aware of God's prevenient grace. As St Paul says, we are called as Christians to work out our own salvation in fear and trembling. We can nevertheless do so with confidence because it is God who is at work in us, enabling us to will and to work for his good pleasure.[8]

All Christian theologians, Methodists especially, affirm that to 'have faith' involves more than mere assent to propositions. The Christian who affirms faith in the words of the creed, 'I believe in God, Father, Son and Holy Spirit' knows that when said with conviction the words require a life which is informed by conversation with the Christian story. But this is easier said than done. Many a Methodist preacher will remind his congregation Sunday by Sunday that the standards of Christian thinking and Christian behaving to which they are called are those which are informed by the mind of Christ, whereas frequently the behaviour of Christians and the pronouncements of the Church are trimmed to accommodate the conventional wisdom of the prevailing culture.

The phenomenal expansion of Methodism in America, combined with the enormous prosperity of Methodists led in the nineteenth century to an uncritical attitude to the morality of business and politics. Preachers opposed greed, injustice and indifference to the welfare of others, but the very virtues they encouraged, sobriety, industry and self-discipline, stimulated the development of individualistic market capitalism. Moreover, it was easy to confuse the desire for personal salvation with self-reliance and individual prosperity. Something similar happened in England. As the Methodist historian, David Hempton says, 'Methodism, it seemed, had arrived at somewhere near the centre of middle class culture by the third quarter of the nineteenth century.'[9]

Stanley Hauerwas (b. 1940) urges Methodists now to give their theological language a sharp edge so as to 'make a difference'.[10] For Hauerwas, that means the Church must be the faithful community, informed by the mind of Christ. He believes that Methodism acquired political influence, compromised with the politico-economic-military machine of the state and supported the *status quo*. It lost its prophetic voice and succumbed to the irrelevant comfortable complacency of 'civil religion'.

The Church's primary role, enshrined in 1950s Methodism was to support those who think they run the world. In contrast I wanted a church capable of reminding those who think they run the world, that they are deluded.[11]

Theology is not reducible to ethics: but theological enquiry and moral endeavour are inextricable. Hauerwas put his ecclesiology and his moral perspective succinctly – the Church embodies the witness of Christ and tells the Christian story in its life and teaching.

V

Christ, the Light of the World

Christians have often been puzzled about who Christ is and what he does: Christological controversy not infrequently divides the Church. There are classic statements in the creeds and in official confessions of the Church which emerged through debate in the first centuries of the Church.[12] It is vital to wrestle with their meaning in order to work out what his life and work now mean for Christians and for the world. Answers insofar as there are any, are many and complex. This is not necessarily a bad thing because it provides a healthy stimulus to careful reflection as we face up to the many issues raised for faith and the well-being of human society by our contemporary culture(s).

In an attempt to take responsibility for their understanding of Christ Methodist theologians have attended to scripture, involved themselves with the conversation about him between the generations of believers and done so with awareness of the evolution of cultural themes. Historians questioned the historical record; philosophers puzzled about the sense of theological claims; scientists questioned the credibility of the miracles. But while debating the meaning and implications of the person of Christ, Methodist theology remains true to the tradition into which Wesley had introduced it and affirmed his human and divine nature. Christ in his humanity calls his disciples to engage as they were able with the interests, concerns, insights and opportunities of the society in which they found themselves. Christ in his divinity called his disciples to enter his vision of the world of humankind as adopted children of God. Their attempt to put this into practice could take many forms. But it involved a prayerful attempt to enter into the mind of Christ so that, by obeying Christ's Great Commandment

123

they would increasingly 'love the Lord their God with all their heart, with all their soul, and with all their mind and their neighbours as themselves'.[13]

St Paul writes in his letter to the Church at Phillipi, 'Let the same mind be in you that was in Christ Jesus.'[14] The context is Jesus' gracious humility, his obedience to God in accepting death, even death on the cross and God's exaltation of him so that all people will come to confess him Lord, to the glory of God the Father. It would be a mistake to confine this to a 'moral' perspective. Of course it is that, but knowing and loving God so that one wants to do God's will means knowing and loving other people which in turn means hard work and making a deliberate choice. The range of potential responsibilities which this embraces has become clearer as the Methodist Church becomes a part of many societies and many environments across the world.

In America, an expanding population, the move westward and the need to hold communities together led the British theologian Richard Watson (1781–1833) to focus on the Church and personal evangelism; his approach emphasized the revelation of the triune nature of God and God's sovereignty. Nevertheless, he did not believe that God's grace *forced* a response; rather he claimed God's grace was working through justice and goodness and relied on human responsibility for its fulfilment. He did not as a matter of fact have a passionate engagement with the world, but he recognized that human salvation and happiness depended upon the proper exercise of his God-given freedom.

In a more mature period of the Methodist Church in America, Daniel Whedon (1808–1885) had wide influence as editor of the Methodist Quarterly Review; he also emphasized human autonomy. Following Kant, he affirmed

No man is to blame for what he cannot help. Power underlies responsibility.[15]

He agreed that human beings did have the power to accept responsibility, but only by God's grace and if they sought the mind of Christ. As Methodists look around their world there are many disfunctional relationships to challenge – child labour, racial discrimination, the treatment of women, exploitation of the world's resources. They undermine the possibility of establishing a community of persons-in-relation which is compatible with God as he is conceived in his Trinitarian nature. Both Richard Watson and Borden Parker Bowne, for example, were opposed to the slave trade as also was John Wesley, because it was obvious to them ownership of one person by another dehumanized both the owner and the slave.

Methodist theologizing holds together theory and practice. To work at the meaning of the doctrine of the Trinity is at the same time to be curious about its significance for human behaviour. 'What does the triune nature of God mean for us now?' implies the question, 'What must I do to show that I believe it?' An answer might be that the Three Persons in One God are both individuals in their own right *and* indivisibly the unity which is God. So to believe in the Trinity means that I must treat my fellow humans as independent persons in their own right and at the same time strive to make real the one community of humanity and creation. What this implies in theory and in practice involves both intellectual enquiry and moral discipline.

There are dangers. We may be overwhelmed by the experience of the world, or lose touch with the tradition and the foundations of the faith. In order to find ourselves again we may take a fundamentalist stance and affirm the faith with little regard to our actual situation, or alternatively adapt it so that the core of the gospel and its 'meaning' are so diluted by liberal phraseology that we lose both continuity with the tradition and relevance. In either case the gospel is distorted and God-talk (theology) abstracted from engagement with cultural life.

Wesley's example is seminal for us. His primary theological purpose was to affirm the gospel without compromise by bringing it into relationship with the contemporary experience of those whom he met for whom he believed the gospel was intended.[16] Committed as he was to engaging in God's conversation with the world, he determined at the same time to be in conversation with his own society, with its moral challenges and its cultural influences.

In order to do this he reminded himself of the sources of God's conversation with the world in scripture and tradition and what it revealed to human sensibilities about the nature of God and God's relationship with the world. He followed as best he could the theological ideas and development of the Christian story over succeeding centuries. Far from being merely reactive to the personal events of his life, or the social and intellectual circumstances of his time, he went back to the beginning in order to reaffirm the traditional faith and then follow the story through as it developed in order to be able to tell it clearly in his own time.

He might well be described as a traditionalist, provided the term is correctly understood. A traditionalist is not focused on preserving the past for its own sake, by repeating words current at a supposedly privileged historical period; rather a traditionalist is concerned to be so familiar with the circumstances which gave life to particular ideas and practices as to be able to take up the tale for himself and translate them consistently and accurately into current speech. In this way themes are stated and developed so that we continue to make sense of them.

Thus, for example, while Wesley was widely read in the cultural life of his time he was not taken in by it. He took note of what Locke had to say, but was not himself either an empiricist in the sense that he believed the only source of true knowledge to be sense experience, nor was he persuaded that human beings were incapable of following the way of truth. He took experience seriously, and was well-aware that doubt and subsequent enquiry were features of the human condition. However, he held that there was an inherent coherence between the Divine Creator's affectionate concern to communicate himself and the desire of humankind to know God which was perfectly expressed in the person of Jesus Christ.

One might say therefore that the Mind of Christ is a divinely given and therefore lively awareness of the presence and power of God which can inform the whole of a person's attempt to know himself, the world and God. 'Practical Divinity' leads to 'Reasonable Faith'; these two styles of theologizing embrace the mystical tradition including the Greek Orthodox doctrine of divinization, and the reasonable perspective of Aquinas.[17] What we believe and are, we do: what we do is effectively an expression of who we are. That is true for personal life and the life of society worldwide. Wesley felt himself called to 'spread scriptural holiness across the land' – he urged his followers to do the same.

The insights of Methodist theology focus the light of Christ who vivifies our picture of God, Redeemer, Sustainer and Creator: Father, Son and Holy Spirit.

The Mind of Christ: Science and Religion

It is widely held that science has disproved religion. The assumption is therefore that we shall get on better, learn more and faster, be less trammeled by ignorance and less bothered by moral scruples, if we ignore religion and theology. After all, it is true we have no need of that hypothesis, when working in the laboratory: the outcome of an experiment does not depend upon the faith of the scientist.

When theologians treat theology as a self-regulating discipline they encourage a destructive isolationism which may follow, for example, when a School of Theology belongs to but is not thoroughly integrated into the intellectual life of the university. Hauerwas experienced this when theological colleagues met only with theologians, and even took no part in the life of a church. Without open conversation in a 'university', or contact with the 'real' world of Christian community, a person with the title Professor of Theology may be very scholarly, but as Methodism would see it, he or she could not really be a theologian. A Christian theologian is necessarily involved with all aspects of human experience in order to contribute to the conversation which God has begun in creation. Aristotle identified curiosity as a defining feature of what it was to be human: Christians agree and regard the thirst for knowledge as a God-given feature of our humanity which we neglect at our peril. To bury a talent and not to develop it through hard work, is stultifying and, as we see it, will earn the censure of God and man.

Our investigation of the natural world by our God-given powers stimulated by curiosity and informed by intelligent experiment springs from the freedom we feel to engage in it because it is God's world, God's creation to which God is committed. We feel at home in God's world and comfortable in exploring it.

The more we understand God's world and our place in it, the more likely we are, with moral insight, to use what we know to build a world with God in which *shalom* – affectionate concern, happiness, contentment, justice and peace, is enjoyed by all. Scientific enquiry is essential if we intend to care for the world and make good use of it. It is part of the process by which we enter the mind of Christ through whom all things were made.

F. Pratt Green (1903–2000), a distinguished British Methodist minister and hymn writer, celebrates this vision.

It is God who holds the nations in the hollow of his hand;
It is God whose light is shining in the darkness of the land;
It is God who builds his City on the rock and not the sand:
May the living God be praised!

It is God whose purpose summons us to use the present hour;
Who recalls us to our senses when a nation's life turns sour;
In the discipline of freedom we shall know his saving power:
May the living God be praised!

When a thankful nation, looking back has cause to celebrate
Those who win our admiration by their service to the state;
When self-giving is a measure of the greatness of the great:
May the living God be praised!

He reminds us every sunrise that the world is ours on lease:
For the sake of life tomorrow may our love for it increase;
May all races live together, share its riches, be at peace:
May the living God be praised![18]

We must hope so – which means since we are talking of Christian hope, that it only bears fruit if we work for it.

VII

The Creation

To interpret enquiry into the nature of our world as a missionary enterprise may seem odd. But love of the world is a key ingredient to our service of our fellow human beings, both now and in the future.

The world is not 'over there', apart from us and operating independently of us; its health affects our well-being. What we do as part of it has an influence upon the rest of it: as we are increasingly aware.

Of course, even to call the world a creation raises serious issues. To take but one aspect – the perennial problem of theodicy. J. L. Mackie claims that the theist is required to believe, but cannot do so with logical consistency, that God is omnipotent, omniscient and wholly good, and that evil exists.[19] There is surprisingly no distinctive major discussion of the problem in Methodist theological literature partly, I suspect, because Methodists believe God has overcome evil.

Standing consciously or unconsciously in the tradition of Augustine and Aquinas, Methodists believe that evil (or to use the theological term 'sin') is the consequence of misusing our God-given freedom. Yet notwithstanding the fact of sin, God's prevenient grace affirms the presence of God with his world, a presence confirmed in Christ who provides the 'cure' for sin, so the person of faith can be happy knowing that by God's grace, salvation is available for all.

There is no magic here; it presumes a sacrificial willingness on the part of God to accept responsibility for the work he has begun in creation and on the part of human being and human society, to share responsibility. Only thus can one know that one is saved. An analogy from education is pertinent. However good the teacher, the pupil will learn nothing unless he puts his mind to it though, of course, the good teacher will work hard to win the pupil's support and show that he is capable of learning: she will sit with him, encouraging him and never taking 'no' for an answer. Above all, the teacher will demonstrate by her attitude that the world is good, that it responds to love and to courteous attention. So also with God. In creating, God provides an environment in which the fullness of life may be enjoyed by all humankind. But in order to do so, each human being has to commit himself, body, mind and soul, to the task of making it so. And as with the teacher so with God as Christians understanding him: God sits encouragingly alongside each human person. And the root of that encouragement is the biblical perception that, 'God sees to it that the world is good', that it responds to love and courteous attention and is our home where we can come to know God and therefore the truth about ourselves and the world. Indeed by so doing, God in Christ, as Christians say, overcomes the world.

This raises a plethora of issues associated with the relationship of God and the world. For example, how does the development of our scientific understanding of the world impact upon our theological enquiring? It is interesting that despite the controversy arising from the publication of Darwin's *Origin of Species* (1859) there is little if any reference to its influence on Methodist theology. In *The Oxford Handbook of Methodist Studies* there are only two marginal allusions to Darwin and no substantial discussion of Darwinism.[20]

There are two possible reasons for this. First, Methodism laid great emphasis upon the importance of personal experience as the ground of faith and was more impressed by the interior life than evidence from outside. In America, Nathan Bangs' theological perspective summed up the environment in which American Methodism received *The Origin of Species*. The key features of his theology were two, the Holy Spirit and the grace of God. The Holy Spirit inspired and confirmed personal experience; the grace of God encouraged the search for salvation and assured the faithful believer of God's presence with him or her. He refuted absolutely predestination: it was inconsistent with the experience of believers who know God's gracious presence and believe in the power of God's love to save humankind utterly from all sin and iniquity.

Secondly, when the influence of Darwinism might have been thought likely to make a destructive impact, Methodist theology in America (as opposed to England) was dominated by the German philosophical tradition of personal idealism which made it easier to evade the controversy over evolutionary theory. William F. Warren (1833–1929), Borden Parker Bowne (1847–1910) (both of whom studied in Germany) together with Edgar S. Brightman (1884–1953) were largely responsible for the development of Boston personalism. Brightman believed that philosophy and theology must be open-ended because they had to cope with the constantly changing world of human experience. Brightman regarded God as real and finite and therefore limited in his control of affairs at any given time, but ultimately triumphant because of his personal commitment to overcome evil.

The personalist school claimed that the sum of human experience was best explained by the assumption that at the heart of the universe there is God, the supreme value, personal, uncreated but eternally creative. The position aroused much controversy: Bowne, for example, was accused of heresy. His thinking about the relation of God and the world, it was suggested, left no room for two essential features of orthodox theology, namely miracles, and the substitutionary theory of the atonement. Moreover his version of 'personalism' seemed to some to question belief in the Trinity.

In fact Bowne conceived the notion of God 'intervening' in a world from which he was 'absent' to be unchristian. His theistic naturalism assumed the immanent activity of God in the world through God's gracious personal presence and through persons at all times and in all places. His view is consistent with the doctrine of prevenient grace, which itself implies that the conception of God's 'intervention' in the world is a mistake, since he is eternally present in his creation. Bowne's acquittal by a council of Methodist bishops in 1904 confirmed the liberal perspective of Methodist theology in America which lasted until the middle of the twentieth century.

Existentialism was another route whereby the force of evolutionary theory was deflected. Carl Michalson (1915–1965), talked of historical existence as being the vehicle of meaning which implied, as far as he was concerned, the irrelevance of looking for reality *per se* – there was no such thing. In this way he believed, God had in Christ released humanity from the limitations of scientific understanding which would otherwise limit the significance of the world of personal relationships.[21]

But something had to be said more directly about the relationship of science and religious belief. Charles Coulson, a distinguished Methodist scientist, delivered the John Calvin McNair Lectures at North Carolina University in 1955.[22] He is sometimes credited with inventing the phrase 'god-of-the-gaps', a view which he held to be obvious nonsense. How could God explain what science could not yet explain if he did not also account for those things which science did apparently explain? God, as Christians conceived him must account for everything or for nothing. Bowne had evinced absolute confidence in the rationality of the world and the unity of truth; Coulson did also. However, Coulson and Herbert

Butterfield, a Methodist historian, were also clear that the 'scientific revolution' of the sixteenth and seventeenth centuries onwards implied as significant a shift in our understanding of God and God's relationship with the world, as the Renaissance and the Reformation.[23] It raised unavoidable questions.

Coulson toyed with the idea of complementary explanations adducing several examples from science and ordinary life to illustrate his theory: science and theology were perhaps two languages which provided the tools to talk about different aspects of experience. However, while there may in certain cases be complementary explanations of human experience, they must be in some way related: truth is essentially one in God's creation. Better perhaps, to re-examine the neglected contribution of metaphysics to our framework of understanding. We hypothesize about our physical experience in explanatory systems, test them by experiment, review the results and, where necessary, reshape the original explanation. But behind this process are assumptions which are integral to it whose examination lies in the field of metaphysics. Metaphysics is not independent of the physical world; it is inherent within it and accounts for the sense of responsibility we feel for the exercising personal judgement as we form the 'knowledge' we have and the uses to which we put it.

Bernard Lonergan S. J. (1904–1984) is helpful here. He had three imperatives which he believed we should keep in mind in the task of explanation: be attentive, be intelligent, be responsible.[24] Careful attention to these was necessary if we were to acquire a growing body of knowledge on which we could rely. The explanation of the relevance of these commands, he suggested, was that behind all of our experience lay the rational, coherent and personal reality of God, with whom we were in conversation. I think Coulson would have found this approach deeply satisfying given that he and Lonergan shared a vast stretch of scientific and mathematical experience.

The issues raised by science for theology are not simply for scholars; they concern every Christian. Wesley was keen to educate his itinerant preachers and through them all Methodists. A remarkable British Methodist minister, The Rev'd Bill Gowland (1911–1991), accepted an analogous challenge. He was a well-known preacher, concerned for the poor and exploited, who latterly worked as an industrial chaplain. After retirement he turned his missionary eye to science and religion establishing in partnership with leading scientists, *Christ and the Cosmos*. It provided an annual opportunity for puzzled but interested Christians to engage in conversation with distinguished theologians, philosophers and scientists. It flourished for some twenty-five years and is now incorporated into *The Science and Religion Forum*, an interdenominational society which is both a forum for intellectual enquiry and 'missionary' enterprise intent upon engaging the world in conversation with God.

VIII

Conclusion

To enter into the mind of Christ and to seek to do his will involves attending to the world of human relations, personal, communal, national, etc., and asking how the Christian can live his life so as to bear witness to God's way of truth, day in and day out. It also involves loving the creation for its own sake and for God's sake, so as to understand it and use our knowledge redemptively as part of the *mission dei*. In order to do this we are called to understand our world in all its dimensions and our relationship with it. 'The earth is the Lord's and the fullness thereof' – and Methodists mean it.

The celebration of God's presence with God's people in God's world is one way of describing the sacramental life. It involves careful listening and hoping, an appreciation of the role of language in human enquiry and conversation. Learning to read scripture is at the heart of Methodist theology.

Chapter 8

Listening and Hoping

I

Introduction

The Methodist theological emphasis on personal salvation means taking up for oneself – in the Christian community – the conversation which God initiated with his world in creation. It consists of listening, thinking, obeying, testing, believing and hoping. These are not independent activities which we then have to bring together; they are integral facets of the single coherent business of learning to love God. They are the ways in which we enter into the story of faith to say it and live it. I use the word 'say' advisedly because it is associated with the language of scripture. The Hebrew root *dbr (dabar)* means both 'saying' and 'doing': it implies that to 'say' something is at one and the same time to 'do' something and that to 'do' something is at one and the same time to 'say' something. 'Saying' without 'doing' is meaningless: 'Saying' is 'Doing'.

Interestingly, the British philosopher J. L. Austin in his William James Lectures at Harvard in 1955 explores this dimension of the way language works.[1] 'To say' something is not simply to state something, properly understood it is what Austin refers to as 'performative' because of its illocutionary force. Examples would be, 'I do' spoken in a marriage service, or 'I promise to arrive on time.' When we say, 'I give you my word', we express the intention to do something. Jeremiah was invited by the Lord, 'Come, go down to the potter's house and there I will let you hear my words.' What in fact Jeremiah *hears* the Lord saying is what the potter is doing as he makes a mess of one piece of clay on the wheel and chooses to make it into something else. The word of the Lord is the potter's action.[2]

The Bible embodies this insight into language use when talking of God's speech. Metaphorical the language may be, but unreal it is not: it is revelatory. When God 'speaks' God is doing something not, as we might say, simply passing the time of day – though in one sense to pass the time of day is an act because it acknowledges or establishes a relationship.

When the Bible refers to God 'speaking', it signifies the way God involves himself with the world. The Israelites believed that in speaking the world into being God had established a relationship with it. Indeed he had spoken not only the world into existence – which they therefore recognized to be a creation and not a happenstance – but *their* world into existence. And as Christians see it from their own theological perspective, God calls them in Christ to work with him to bring the world to perfection. When God speaks he is through the Word, creating, redeeming and confirming his presence with his people as the Creation story in the Old Testament and the Transfiguration in the New Testament 'say'.[3]

John Wesley and all subsequent Methodist theology hold together in one perspective faith and practice, theology and ethics; by this they show that they have grasped what it means to confess faith in God. To say the words, 'I believe in God', is not merely to own up to a private state of mind, they confess a personal attitude to God, to the world and to other people: they at one and the same time 'perform' one's active response to living in a world which is only properly understood when it includes God.

Listening, thinking, obeying, believing and hoping are dimensions of one process implicit in the response of the children of Israel to the word of Yahweh in the Old Testament, and of the disciples to the Word of God in Christ in the New Testament. Their experience is written up in the many literary forms of scripture, – myth, history, law, prophecy, poetry, wisdom literature, gospel and epistle but where they are significant they constitute one exploration into the meaning of faith.

Scripture is not an historical 'record', though from time to time the accounts may allude to events in order to anchor the Word of God in history and stimulate curiosity about its meaning. Thinking about God's presence and what it means, can lead to dead-ends, brilliant insights, cautious development or unthinking obedience and destruction. But all is honestly put down in the text of scripture: nothing is hidden whether striking visions, false trails, real hopes, mistaken ambitions, genuine faith. Everything is built into the developing conversation begun by God with the world and humankind in creation. Not even entry into the Promised Land is the end, it is a new beginning: the Israelites await the Messiah who will heal all wounds, calm all fears and deliver peace and justice to all creation.

For Christians the conversation is focused in God's revelation of himself in his Word, Jesus Christ, who is no terminus either. He is an expression of the eternal conversation of God with his creation, which the Church, the Body of Christ, is called to continue and embody. The resurrection of Christ reveals – 'says' – in dramatic form the dynamic nature of God as he is in himself, a lively, life-giving, eternally gracious presence. All our Christian hope, all encouragement of faith, all stimulus of thoughtful enquiry about human flourishing, is grounded in God, Father, Son and Holy Spirit.

II

Joining In: Thinking with God – Not About God

I believe that the book of Deuteronomy represents a style of theologizing analogous to the way in which Methodists approach theology. Deuteronomy is a law book informed by the prophetic vision. In its present editorial form it came into existence around the middle of the sixth century B.C., the product of a reform movement among the Israelites. It illuminates their contemporary situation by retelling the story of Moses and putting in clear language the moral demands of their covenant relationship with Yahweh. God would never go back on his commitment to them; they would never be released from the covenant, the very foundation of their liberty. The text has no identifiable individual author; it emerges from conversation and argument over a long time incorporating the experience of 'professional' people, communities and families as they struggled to understand their history. It offered them a future.

The final draft as we have it may have been put together by levitical priests unattached to the Temple and therefore with more freedom than would otherwise have been the case with the Temple hierarchy. This may be no more than informed speculation: it cannot be confirmed since we know little about the levitical priesthood at this time. However, as a committed community of faith scattered around the countryside they would have been in a good position to know the condition of national life, and would be likely to have had a concern for its welfare.

The story of the Exodus as retold in Deuteronomy makes the point well that listening, thinking, obeying, believing and hoping are key features of a lively faith community. The Israelites hear the word of God through Moses; they think about what he says God intends to do, they obey, believe and set out in hope. The people, as they believe and continue to remind themselves who they are, are brought out of Egypt by the power of God's almighty hand. What the real historical events were which led to their freedom we know not; clearly some leader whom we call 'Moses' had a vision, the skill to communicate it and a determination 'to make a difference'. He gave his partners in exile a new sense of themselves as sons of Abraham, the covenant people, and motivated them to get on their feet and challenge the Egyptian authorities. This they did; they entered anew into their inheritance as the people of Yahweh and marched to liberty in The Promised Land.

The Israelites were puzzled as they reflected upon their freedom. How had it come about? It was certainly not attributable to their efforts or explained by the incidental fact that they happened to be more numerous than their enemies. They were not as a matter of fact a large body. They were sufficiently self-aware, too, to recognize that they had not earned God's blessing because they were morally superior to other people: on the contrary, they knew they were not; they were frequently dispirited and disobedient. But implicit in this assumption is an intuitive insight, perhaps unique among the peoples surrounding them, that Yahweh's inner nature was characterized by moral qualities and that he demanded the same capacity for sound judgement of those who were in relationship with him.

So why were they free? Because they believed quite simply, as Moses told them, that God had chosen them for no other reason than that he had chosen them. What is more, Moses warned them, they were not to presume upon it in the future. They needed to remember that this was a long-standing commitment of God; God had established a covenant with them. God had made promises to their Fathers, Abraham, Isaac and Jacob and their children for ever: in redeeming them from captivity in Egypt he had honoured the covenant. Moreover God would always keep his covenant promise because they were the object of his undeviating, absolutely consistent and eternal loving-kindness. Paradoxically, that meant even more especially that they *could* not presume upon it without suffering consequences.

To be loved by God is to share a relationship which involves God's commitment of himself and our listening and obeying. To be disobedient is to invite the fire of judgement for to remove oneself from the love of God is to attempt the impossible and to render oneself liable to be scorched by the same love. We vaguely know something of that in human relationships, especially in the relation of parents and children. Good parents never cease to love their children, whatever they do; when children betray that love and come to themselves they realize what they have cost their parents, are mortified and, metaphorically, 'scorched with fire'.

In order to join in the telling of the story of God's relationship with God's world and humankind one has to learn to listen: it is like listening to music. One has to learn how to pay attention so as to identify the themes, recognize the form and follow the development yet, at the same time one has to hear it 'whole'. Listening to a symphony or a string quartet is a physical experience but unless one enters into it wholeheartedly with some knowledge of where it sits in the history of music, and how it relates to current 'experiments', one will not 'hear' or be able personally to interpret it and add to the development of the tradition. Moses is only too well aware that to 'hear' requires that one tells the story. So Moses addresses the people,

Hear, O Israel, The Lord our God is our God, the Lord alone. You shall love the Lord your God with all your heart, and with all your soul, and with all your might. Keep these words which I am commanding you today in your heart. Recite them to your children and talk about them when you are at home and when you are away, when you lie down and when you rise.[4]

Listening to God's word must never stop: the possibility of obedience only remains a present reality as one continues to give attention to God. So, the editors of Deuteronomy, no doubt remembering past experience, warn the Israelites that entry into a land flowing with milk and honey will bring both opportunities and threats to the well-being of their community.

> Take care that you do not forget the Lord your God, by failing to keep his commandments, his ordinances, and his statutes, which I am commanding you this day.[5]
>
> Do not say to yourself, 'My power and the might of my hand have gained me this wealth.' But remember the Lord your God, for it is he who gives you power to get wealth, so that he may confirm his covenant that he swore to your ancestors, as he is doing today. If you do forget the Lord your God and follow other gods to serve and worship them, I solemnly warn you today that you shall surely perish.[6]
>
> Justice, and only justice, you shall pursue, so that you may live and occupy the land that the Lord your God is giving you.[7]

Deuteronomy holds together theology and ethics; they are inseparable. If you will only remember God, listen to him, think through what you hear, obey, believe and act in hope, you will prosper and live enjoyably in the land God is giving you. Provided, of course, you always keep in mind the possibility that you can misinterpret your experience and make false judgements!

Listening and hoping implies, as far as the Bible is concerned in both Old and New Testaments, that in the quietness of our own hearts and in the roar of life, God's voice can be heard and his will done. Indeed on that both our present and future well-being will depend, because only then shall humanity live with the grain of the universe. There's plenty on which to build too – all the witnesses present their evidence and tell their stories: Abraham, Isaac and Jacob, Moses and Elijah, the historians and prophets, wisdom teachers and leaders of worship in the Old Testament.

The New Testament continues the theme in telling the story of Jesus through the responses of the apostles and the disciples, thinkers and writers, men and women and all the worshipping church communities which we find scattered across the Mediterranean world. Jesus, takes up the same conversation, refocuses it and takes it so seriously, in his 'speaking and doing' that all but a few of his contemporaries see him as a threat to their fragile prosperity. But the judgement which Jesus offers is no more than the working out again of the covenant which God had established with Abraham, Isaac and Jacob. God fulfils that promise indelibly and inevitably in Jesus' Crucifixion and Resurrection, the outcome of Jesus' listening, reflecting, obeying, believing and hoping. The beginnings, middles, ends and futures of their listening and hoping are celebrated here and constitute an invitation to take up the story for ourselves. The new Exodus has taken place; the Promised Land – the Kingdom of God is established but if it is to be enjoyed for real then we have actually to take up the story for ourselves. But what or who are we listening to and what are we hoping for? The future is beyond our grasp, but paradoxically, it may be said, within reach, because the past, present and future are God.

III

Listening and Hoping

Methodist theology has inherited a developing understanding of God and now works at its meaning in order to explore what we believe, and learn what is involved in Christian living. The concern is theological and ethical. The conversation of the Methodist Church in its various national Conferences, district and circuit meetings, among groups of ordinary members attempts to add to and deepen awareness of God's presence in creation, in Christ and in his Church. In the process they will take account of their roots, their historical experience as a society, a Movement and a church.

Taking account of their contemporary circumstances they will to the limit of their ability both absorb and question the insights of the natural sciences together with their technical applications. They will engage with social scientists, economists and politicians in order as best they can to share responsibility for and contribute to public debate about the well-being of our future society. We want to know what it all adds up to *theologically* – that is for our understanding of God – so that our worldwide Methodist society is equipped to live a life of faith in conformity with the tradition of faith into which it has entered. What does our behaviour 'say' that we are hoping for and actually striving to achieve?

Christian hope is not an impotent wish for an impossible future. It is the attempt in the light of as full an appreciation as we can muster of the actual circumstances of human existence, to make judgements in full confidence that the future can be more just and therefore in a significant sense better than the past – for everyone and for the whole creation. The dynamism built into our thinking does not simply come from the application of human intelligence and blind optimism – let alone any belief that we are more numerous or more morally well-behaved than others – it is based upon a sense of call, the faith that we can work with the God of Abraham, Isaac and Jacob, the Father of Our Lord, Jesus Christ for the perfecting of his creation.

IV

A Real Presence

At this point I return to consideration of the doctrine of prevenient grace: as Methodists engaged in the business of thinking theologically, the doctrine underpins our way of thinking and our approach to life. Whenever we listen and wherever we look at our experience of one another and of the world, we expect to find God. Nothing that we do *makes* God present because we have no power over God, but almost anything that we do can make us aware of God's presence. In this sense, Methodists know what it means to talk about and celebrate the real presence. And on that we build.

As St. Paul says:

If God is for us, who is against us? He who did not withhold his own Son, but gave him up for all of us, will he not with him also give us everything else?

> I am convinced that neither death, nor life, nor angels,
> nor rulers, nor things to come, nor powers, nor height, nor
> depth, nor anything else in all creation, will be able to
> separate us from the love of God in Christ Jesus our Lord.[8]

The Methodist conversation with God is real; it is engaged in
with an intense urgency, but like everyone else Methodists are
open to self-deception and complacency. When that happens we
are driven back, like the editors of Deuteronomy, to tell the story
from the beginning and follow it through until we can take up the
threads again for ourselves. This has implications for the way
Methodists approach worship as we shall see in the next chapter.
A Deuteronomic reform is required. But where do we begin? For
Methodists the answer is straightforward – with the Bible: this is
why learning to read the Bible is basic to Methodist theology.

V

The Authority of Scripture: The Response of Preachers

Listening to scripture – to learn, mark and inwardly digest it –
means attending to the text and attempting to understand it.
Methodists have always been readers of scripture; John Wesley's
preaching and Charles Wesley's hymns are based upon it. The conversation of the class meeting was informed by scripture. The
result is that, certainly since the beginning of the twentieth century, Methodists have been in the forefront of biblical scholarship.
John Wesley preceded the birth of critical biblical scholarship.
Nevertheless, in his own way he was thoughtful and intelligent
in the way he approached it. He appears to have kept abreast of
the latest readings of the text and engaged with diverse interpretations when he found himself in difficulty. He was anxious that his
preaching genuinely expounded the text *and* effectively commended the gospel. He would not have understood any distinction
between the two: as a preacher you should no more exploit the
text than you should the congregation.

He believed he was assisted by the Holy Spirit when he attended to the Word of God in scripture and sought the truth. He sought the truth hidden in the text, not an interpretation imposed upon it by personal prejudice. One scholar has dismissed the sermons as 'primarily a string of biblical quotations'.[9] This is to do John Wesley an injustice. Certainly he unquestioningly assumed the truth of miracles,[10] the Virgin Birth and the physical resurrection of Christ; in doing so, however, he was in his opinion affirming both their reasonableness and their testimony to the revelation of God. His published sermons have been so worked on that they lack the potency they presumably had when preached 'live'. But he did all that he could to encourage Methodists to read the Bible for themselves.

New ways of approaching the Bible were required from the nineteenth century onwards when the hitherto generally accepted position on biblical inspiration and the nature of revelation had been brought into question by textual analysis, the emergence of historical criticism and Darwinism. It became much harder to defend cogently the apparently 'obvious', meaning of scripture. Actually, the tradition presents many styles of reading the text. Augustine and Origen, for example, were attentive to literal meaning, but both recognized the importance of moral and especially allegorical approaches. This is clear from their sermons and commentaries. Wesley who was well read in the Early Church Fathers will have been familiar with these.

The first reaction of Methodist theologians to the challenges was carefully conservative. Richard Watson defended the truth as he saw it by, as it were, speaking from inside the bubble of the Church and therefore evading some of the tough questions. He asserted the authority of God and the superiority of revelation to reason. W. B Pope followed something of the same line; he focused upon the revelation of God in Jesus Christ and did not engage seriously with either Darwinism or the new historical criticism. Hugh Price Hughes was conservative too, in his reading of scripture, but he took his firm acceptance of the bible-based doctrine of the Fatherhood of God from the Church into the world and gave Methodism's social concern a major position in British public life.

In America Milton S. Terry (1864–1914) and Hinckley G. Mitchell (1846–1920) took a new direction. They approached the Bible as they would any other book in order to investigate its provenance, the source of its ideas, its chronology and textual integrity. They held that the meaning which they discerned by employing these new techniques was vouchsafed to them as the gift of the Holy Spirit but this hardly recommended itself to those who questioned the reasonableness of any approach to scripture which took seriously the higher criticism being developed by German scholars.

Matters came to a head when Mitchell questioned the Mosaic authorship of the Pentateuch, showing quite clearly that the five books were the editorial product of a plethora of disparate material put together over several hundred years. He was charged with heresy in 1895. The dispute in which he was supported by Bowne his Boston University colleague lasted until his eventual acquittal in 1905.

Since the beginning of the twentieth century, the full range of critical approaches has been generally assumed to be an essential tool for exploring scripture. But whereas in America Methodist theology has developed in relation to philosophical schools, in Britain the basis has been biblical scholarship. This may have been due to the fact that doctrine was largely uncontroversial; it was assumed to overlap if not to be actually identical with the Established Church. Methodist theological energy concentrated on the Bible, on listening to the word of God, thinking through the implications of new analyses of scripture and learning to obey it.

Professor Sarah Heaner Lancaster, of the Methodist Theological School in Ohio, Delaware puts the Methodist approach to scripture admirably when she writes,

> Our tradition has understood that knowledge of God has powerful experiential effects, so we have long felt that something is at stake in the way we understand God's communication to us.
>
> If there is anything distinctive about a Methodist understanding of Scripture and revelation, it will be found in this connection between knowledge and life.[11]

What this led to can be variously seen in the lives of some influential British Methodist ministers of the twentieth century. John Scott Lidgett and Donald Soper (Lord Soper), for example, were both deeply rooted in the Bible from which emanated their passion for social reform and political involvement. Neither of them was inclined to a conservative position in theology though both considered themselves orthodox. Each treated scripture as inspired; they believed close attention to it would reveal the truth about God and God's salvation of the world through Christ, but this was not a simple matter. To discern the truth one had to attend to the text with one's whole self. Their attitude could from time to time get them into trouble with those of a more conservative persuasion. Indeed when in 1959 Lord Soper preached at Ballymena in Northern Ireland Ian Paisley, threw a Bible at him because he denied its literal truth.[12]

Lidgett and Soper took Methodism into the heart of public life – Donald Soper was a member of the House of Lords – because they believed on the basis of reading the Bible that salvation was personal not individualistic; public not private. Scott Lidgett's missionary commitment focused on education which he believed the gospel required to be available for all; Soper on the reform of public and personal life. He attacked poverty throughout his life and embraced pacificism and teetotalism.

Two other examples illustrate further the diversity of the British Methodist response to biblical scholarship. William E. Sangster was minister of Westminster Central Hall, in the heart of London from 1939 to 1965 where his example and preaching were an inspiration to thousands during the crisis of the Second World War. He was very widely read, a student of scripture but with a profound interest in philosophy: he was absolutely convinced that Methodism had a unique contribution to bring to the worldwide church. But Methodists seemed to him to have lost confidence in the gospel: the search for holiness had become an irrelevance consequent upon the trauma of war and the disillusioning experience of victory. Sangster wanted Methodists to recover a passion for evangelism and the spiritual life. He was that rare combination of an intellectual, a pastor and a preacher: it was necessary to hold them together, he believed, if the Church was to engage in the conversation with God and enter into the liberty of God's forgiving presence. He would not compromise the gospel as the way of truth, and the promise of personal holiness.

Leslie Weatherhead (1893–1976) sat uneasily within the Methodist Church in some respects and took full advantage of his liberty when in 1936 he became minister of the City Temple, the main Congregational Church in central London. He was nevertheless elected President of the Conference in 1953. His reading of scripture led him to Christ whom he describes as 'endlessly at work in and through man, by all the ways open to love – without coercion, or bribing, or favoritism – to effect a unity, an at-one-ment between man and God'.[13] Having experienced the freedom into which he believed Christ had delivered him, he rejected any authority, school of thought or individual who limited that freedom by calling on authorities outside themselves. He was disinclined to debate with those whose reading of the Bible led them to a different theological position since he did not believe the Bible required belief in particular doctrines. The gospel invited all who would listen to follow Christ and think through what it actually meant to believe in him and to do his will. In order to help people find the truth which possessed them he developed a counseling ministry alongside his preaching which owed something to his experience of Moral Re-Armament and The Oxford Group founded by Frank Buchman (1878–1961) of which he was a member from 1930–1939. In view of his rejection of external authorities, it is paradoxical that critics of his counselling were often able to point to an unhealthy dependence on him on the part of some of his clients.

His book, *The Christian Agnostic*, produced furore: some regarded it as scandalous but to others it came as a profound relief. It did not, as some critics suggested, reduce the Christian Faith to a moral code and the invitation to lead a decent life; rather, it affirmed the undying, indestructible presence of everything that is best as found in Christ. He had a high view of the work of Christ.

His death is a revelation of the nature of God, and a pledge that God will stand by me until I am made one with him.[14]

> [Christ] committed himself to the task of recovering all humanity to God, however long it might take, however arduous the way, however unrewarding the toil.[15]

He rejected unchecked subjectivism as the authority in religion; he believed in the power of prayer, and the need to take all available evidence into account. But he was at best ambiguous in his attitude to the Church.

> Christianity must have a marvelous inherent power or the churches would have killed it long ago.[16]

VI

Biblical Scholarship

The biblical scholarship on which Methodist preaching was based was wide-ranging. It focused to start with on the nitty-gritty of the text and enquiry into the language, its grammar and syntax. W. F. Moulton (1835–1898), the first headmaster of The Leys School, Cambridge, founded in 1878, produced a concordance of the Greek New Testament and shared in the preparation of the New Testament in the *Revised Version* of the Bible (1881).[17] His son, James Hope Moulton (1863–1917), was responsible for a *Prolegomena to a Grammar of the New Testament* and became a Fellow of King's College, Cambridge.

British Methodism may have produced little by way of theological innovation but its influence on theological enquiry grew at one remove as the distinction of Methodist biblical scholarship was recognized by British university theology departments in the course of the twentieth century. The Universities of Manchester, Durham, Birmingham, Oxford, Cambridge, as well as Bangor University College in the University of Wales and Aberdeen University in Scotland, all appointed distinguished Methodist scholars to importance posts. It began with the remarkable contribution of Arthur S. Peake (1865–1929). He reformed the training of ministers during his time as tutor at Hartley College in Manchester where he taught from 1894. He was the first holder of the Rylands

Chair of Biblical Criticism and Exegesis at Manchester University from its incorporation in 1904. Indeed he was the first non-Anglican to hold any theological chair in any British University.

Peake was first and foremost an Old Testament scholar, but he made his most influential contribution to biblical scholarship with the publication of his *Commentary on the Bible* in 1919. It achieved a wide circulation among Protestants and Anglicans. Its success and enormous influence, was partly due to the fact that it was written by a layman, and partly because it was such a comparatively brief one-volume commentary, absolutely up-to-date with regard to the most recent scholarship. The fact that he came from a tradition of Methodism, Primitive Methodism, which was thought to be very conservative in its approach to theology in general and scripture in particular meant that he was trusted even when he took, what to many, was a radical approach. He was largely responsible for the ease with which British Methodism came to accept the results of historical and textual criticism. Most if not all Methodist ministers – certainly in Britain – would have had a copy of the commentary on their shelves. It remained the major resource for preachers both lay and ordained, until a revised edition was produced in 1962 by Professor Matthew Black, a successor of Peake to his chair in the University of Manchester.

Peake was followed by many others; significantly, Norman Snaith, Christopher North and George Anderson in the Old Testament; C. Kingsley Barrett, Kenneth Grayston, James Dunn and Morna Hooker in the New. Morna Hooker had the distinction to be elected to the Lady Margaret Chair in the University of Cambridge, the first layperson and the first woman. Their critical sharpness, linguistic and analytical skills were combined with gifts of interpretation and exegesis which opened up the Bible in ways that the Methodist Church found supportive of their confidence in God's promises.

Study of the Bible drew attention to the range of responses to God implicit in the thinking of both the' Old and New Testaments. James W. Dunn pointed to the theological diversity of the New Testament and the vigorous conversation which was engaged in as they struggled to grasp the truth about Jesus whom they called the Christ. But at no stage did scholars waver in their belief that Christians, however divided the Church seemed to be in current experience, were one in Christ and called to make a reality of it in the world.

VII

Methodist Ecumenism

God is indivisible. In giving himself to the world in the creation and in Christ, it is the wholeness of God who is revealed, not an aspect of God. In the Holy Spirit, active within the world and in the Church, it is the whole of God who is at work. In the Church, the Body of Christ, it is God, Father, Son and Holy Spirit, whom we know and who gives us life and hope, and leads us in the way of truth. The sadness of division is therefore very hard to cope with: the search for unity is a natural consequence of reading scripture and integral to all Methodist theology. Indeed 'ecumenical' is the perspective which best expresses the life and hope of Methodism and informs its theological enquiring.

In order to free themselves to think theologically, the British and American Methodist churches have done their best to heal the divisions which emerged following the death of John Wesley in 1791. The Methodist Church of Great Britain is a union effected in 1932 of three traditions of Methodist churchmanship, Wesleyan, Primitive and United Methodist (itself a coming together of United Methodist Free Churches, with Methodist New Connexion and the Bible Christians). In America the process was analogous: division and ultimate reunion. In 1830 The Methodist Protestant Church separated from the Methodist Episcopal Church over the role of the laity; the Methodist Episcopal Church divided into a northern and a southern grouping in 1844 over disputes about slavery and the power of bishops; they united again in 1939 when they came together with the Methodist Protestant Church to form The Methodist Church. In turn this body joined in 1968 with The Evangelical United Brethren Church to form the United Methodist Church of America.

For more than one hundred and fifty years, the Wesleyan Methodist Church and latterly the Methodist Church of Great Britain has sought to reunite itself with the Church of England. From time to time it has seemed possible, even likely, but all attempts have so far proved abortive. They have been dashed over such matters as the role of bishops and the Anglican Church's unwillingness to recognize Methodist ministers as truly ordained. The most recent initiative began in 1995 and led to the signing by the President of the British Methodist Conference and the Archbishop of Canterbury of a *Covenant of Unity*. This does no more than state the obvious, 'both our churches confess in word and life the Apostolic Faith revealed in the Holy Scriptures'. It is hard to see what stimulus this offers towards unity though there have been local celebrations of it which have encouraged some local optimism.

Ecumenical enthusiasm has not been confined to the 'home' churches within the United Kingdom and America, Methodist involvement in theological exploration towards reunification is worldwide. Participation in the foundation of the Church of South India (1947) was a striking innovation since it preceded the formal establishment of the World Council of Churches and united Episcopal and non-episcopal traditions: namely, the Anglican dioceses, the Methodist Church and the United Church.

Both British and American Methodists have been committed to ecumenism from the very beginning and undertaken a prominent role in promoting the search for the unity of the one, holy, catholic and apostolic church. John R. Mott (1865–1955), a Methodist layman from Iowa, worked tirelessly to establish a universal vision for the non-Roman Catholic Churches. He was the President of the World Student Christian Movement and the chair of the important Edinburgh Missionary Conference of 1910 usually regarded as the first move towards the establishment of the World Council of Churches (WCC) in 1948.

Methodism has made contributions far beyond its size to the WCC. Newton Flew, a British Methodist minister, chaired the Faith and Order meetings of 1937 and 1951 which led to the Council statement that the churches 'should not do separately what they can do together'. At first 147 members, the Council now numbers 349, including most Protestant, and Eastern Orthodox Churches. The Roman Catholic Church is not actually a member but has appointed observers since 1961, and most importantly since 1968 has been a full member of the Faith and Order Commission.

Roman Catholic theologians, therefore, took part in the work which led to the most important theological statement made by the Council hitherto, *Baptism, Eucharist and Ministry* which in a judicious manner identifies areas of agreement towards full unity.[18]

Geoffrey Wainwright, Professor of Systematic Theology at Duke University was instrumental in bringing the final text to fruition.[19] He has been a major influence in the deliberations of the WCC and in the bilateral conversations which Methodism has engaged in with Roman Catholicism. In a book in which he draws together material from his ecumenical involvement, he remarks on the naturalness of Methodism's ecumenism.

> . . . a Methodist imbibes ecumenism with his mother's milk: our eighteenth century founder laid out the spirit and themes of a dialogue that is to serve Christian unity, and it is therefore quite natural that Methodists should have played a prominent part in the twentieth century ecumenical movement.[20]

This is a dimension of world-wide Methodism not confined to British and American theologians. General Secretaries of the Council include three Methodists, Philip Potter (1972–1984) from Dominica, Emilio Castro (1985–1992) from Uruguay and Samuel Kobia (2004–2009) from Kenya.

The range of World Methodist Council (WMC) ecumenical activity since 1966 is impressive. Conversation with the Roman Catholic Church progresses: the WMC authorized further dialogue in 2006 stating the ambition of 'full communion in faith, mission and sacramental life'. The important agreement of the Lutheran Church with the Roman Catholic Church on Justification approved in 1999 was recognized by WMC in 2006. Conversations continue with Anglicanism, Lutheran World Federation, the World Alliance of Reformed Churches and the Salvation Army which itself emerged in the nineteenth century from Methodist roots. There are moves to establish dialogues with Orthodoxy and the Pentecostal Churches.

While it is true that the ecumenical movement is lower on the agenda than it used to be it remains central in Methodist theology.

The achievements of the last century should not be underestimated. Moreover, notwithstanding signs of the Vatican's hardening attitude, Cardinal Walter Kasper, the former President of the Pontifical Council for promoting Christian Unity said in a recent interview that his chief regret from his time of office was that he had not brought an agreement on a common communion with Protestants.

Methodist theology is ecumenical and works to make a reality of the unity of the Church; it is also ecumenical in the wider sense of trying to discover where there is common ground with other faiths. At the current time the importance of this theological task can hardly be exaggerated: it is clear that if human society is to flourish in the global environment in which we live, the world faiths must learn to work together in the common interest of the humanity they claim to serve. This will require mutual respect, curiosity to learn from one another, the sharing of wisdom and above all affectionate concern. Methodists are committed to this with regard to African religions, Judaism, Buddhism, Hinduism, Sikhism, Islam and Confucianism.

VIII

Conclusion

The reality of God's presence with God's people is celebrated in the Eucharist. The generous tradition of Methodist theologizing leads naturally, therefore, to a respect for and celebration of God's saving presence, a recognition that all things are made through the Word, that humankind, if it so chooses, can take responsibility with God for creation and work with God for its perfection. It means being obedient to God's word but not blindly; thinking and understanding are necessary preconditions of faithful obedience since the capacity to think intelligently is one of God's most precious gifts.

Certainly Methodist theology is evangelical in the sense that it is concerned to commend the gospel; but it is also sensitive to the insights of persons from other Christian traditions, other religions and none. It is a community of faithful people, thankful that it has been brought into fellowship with Christ, whom to know is perfect freedom.

The focus of Methodist theological enquiry is to bring all things together and offer them to God in Christ, in faith, hope and praise.

Chapter 9

Wesleyan Revival: A Thankful Worshipping Community

I

Introduction

The mid-twentieth century saw Methodism stimulated by a quickening interest in John Wesley's theology. It was, I believe, encouraged partly by the dismissive implications of Logical Positivism on the one hand and more significantly by the emergence of the Ecumenical Movement on the other. The Verification Principle rejected religious language – indeed all metaphysical discourse – as meaningless because it was neither capable of empirical investigation nor true by definition.[1] The foundation of the World Council of Churches in 1948 questioned ecclesial identity.

First, the account of religious language as meaningless challenged Methodist self-understanding: it was false to the experience of Methodists and led to some serious questioning. One theological reaction hardly helped. Thomas Altizer and Robert Hamilton accepted the redundancy of metaphysics and articulated Christian Atheism.[2] The Christian religion, as they saw it, was not concerned with God's existence but with the essential moral nature of the universe: it enshrined the highest ethical standards which human experience had discovered. Indeed, Death of God theology, as it came to be called, claimed that the Christian Faith did not require belief in God. This struck many as ridiculous and Methodists as inconsistent with faith as they experienced it. They went back to the tradition, took up the Christian story in scripture and the creeds and, as it were, tried to 'begin all over again' though of course that is impossible – retelling always involves reshaping in the light of experience. In particular Methodism was thrust back to its founder, John Wesley. He, too, had found himself in a threatening and hostile environment. What had he to say?

Secondly, Methodist theologians found the Ecumenical Movement congenial to their thinking. But it meant that they had to face up to the question 'Who are we and what do we stand for?' In the United States conversations with the Evangelical United Brethren and in Britain the continuing drama of relations with the Church of England had already focused Methodist minds. More broadly, where did Methodism stand in relation to Roman Catholicism, Orthodoxy and Protestantism?

II

The Recovery of Wesleyan Theology

These twin pressures, cultural and ecclesiological, had a profound influence on Methodism: they raised questions about foundations and provoked interest in John Wesley and his theology. Hitherto he had been admired as evangelist, organizer and preacher, not as theologian. Even in Britain, admiration for the role of the Wesley brothers in the Evangelical Movement had tended to blind Methodists to their wider theological insights. Indeed, while he remained an Anglican clergyman to his life's end, he was admired chiefly, if somewhat misleadingly, as the hero who stood up to the arrogance of bishops, in order to bring the gospel to the poor. This caused British Methodist scholars to focus on its historical influence on the wider Church in the United Kingdom, especially on its impact on political and social matters.[3] In America interest in Wesleyan theology was genuinely new since acknowledgement of John Wesley as founder had not led to on-going interest in the man or his theology.

However, if Wesley was seriously to be studied the first requirement was a modern edition of the works. Thomas Jackson's fourteen volumes were valuable but contained only a fraction of Wesley's writings.[4] The approaching bicentenary of John Wesley's death in 1991 provided the stimulus; a group was established in 1960 under the chairmanship of Robert Cushman of Duke University.

Publication began in 1975 and is still in progress but has already been widely influential.[5]

Wesley's theology was found to be orthodox, generously ecumenical and deeply embodied in the tradition. Wesley's breadth of vision was happily matched by the sympathies of those who engaged with the project: faithfully Methodist, but not narrowly so. Albert C. Outler (1908–1989), for example, had published a generous selection of Wesley material with commentary in 1964.[6] He brought to his study of Wesley, extensive knowledge of the Fathers, especially Origen and Augustine, an appreciation of the importance of philosophy with a special interest in the process philosophy of William Hartshorne and a lively sympathy with contemporary Roman Catholic theology, notably Karl Rahner. He attributed his ecumenism to his Methodist upbringing. He had been an observer at Vatican II and also a member of the Faith and Order Committee of the WCC. He did not share the suspicion of traditional theological language which characterized liberal theologians. Geoffrey Wainwright should be included in the same perspective. He found his orthodox theology with its focus on the Trinity, sacramental worship, ecumenism, passion for justice and pastoral concern all confirmed within the theology of John Wesley.

Richard Heitzenrater (1961–2007) became General Editor of the Bicentennial Edition of John Wesley's works in succession to Frank Baker. He too had wide interests and experience. He de-coded Wesley's personal diaries thereby illuminating the real Mr. Wesley. He used his scholarship to inform the theological debates of the United Methodist Church during the 1980s and chaired the committee responsible for the doctrinal statement in Part II of the Book of Discipline. Following Wesley, Heitzenrater believed that the Church should focus the gospel on current problems facing the world. As an earnest of this he worked after retirement in Eastern Europe with Methodist congregations linked to United Methodism. He explored their relationship with Orthodoxy and developed with them ways in which they could express the transforming power of Methodist spirituality in their respective challenging environments. What shape should their ecclesiology take?

Heitzenrater's concern with the churches of the east was not original. Wesley's interest in the Eastern Fathers is well known: less well known is the contribution of Methodism to ecumenical relations with Orthodoxy. Heitzenrater followed in the footsteps of Methodists such as John Mott (1865–1955). As an earnest of his conviction that the future of the Church in the world depended upon healing of this awful division Mott gave $5,000 of his own money in 1925 towards the purchase of property to begin the Orthodox Theological seminary in Paris for the exiled Russian Orthodox community. Mott's initiative was extremely far-sighted and valuable in promoting ecumenical conversation. The first Dean and Professor of Dogmatic Theology was Sergius Bulgakov who had been expelled from Russia in 1923. A committed, albeit critical ecumenist, Bulgakov helped to establish the Fellowship of St Alban and St Sergius in 1928, to encourage the mutual understanding of the Eastern and Western traditions. Bulgakov talked of the Church as 'God's Grace' and this seemed to Heitzenrater to offer real opportunities for conversation with Methodism given Wesley's own distinctive theology of grace.

Theodore Runyon (Candler School of Theology, Emory University), added a serious 'practical' dimension to the study. He made his most important contribution to Wesleyan theology in response to an invitation of the United Methodist Church General Board for Higher Education and Ministry to provide material for courses of theology, history and social action.[7] Runyon subtly holds together the Wesleyan discussion of theology and ethics and expounds their significance for the practical business of evangelism in the contemporary church. To accept Wesleyan theology today, he urges, means sharing in the dynamic love that recognizes God's presence in creation, acknowledges the sin which blinds humankind to him, finds the redemption of the world through Christ who embodies God's forgiving presence and is inspired by the eschatological vision of The New Creation. The whole story impacts upon the Church's response to human rights, the care of women, the environment and ecumenism among other matters of concern. Runyon develops a relation between the dynamic of Wesley's practical theology and the present interest in liberation theology.[8] He argues that by freeing Wesley from the suspicion of an emphatic focus on individual salvation, his theology is revealed as concerned with the whole work of God in creation.

Robert Cushman (1913–1993) questioned the adequacy of the liberal approach to the tradition: his emphasis was pastoral. He was deeply rooted in the study of philosophy: in a book which he wrote on Plato he celebrated Plato's testimony to the soul's desire for ultimate fulfilment. This deep desire of the human spirit was the ground of a developing sense of sin a dimension of human experience which he believed liberal theologians had neglected. In fact it is man's awareness of sin which is the condition of human reconciliation with God and with himself. The experience of God is God-given and not natural: it depends upon the *felix culpa* of sin. For Cushman Christology is the centre of theology. Jesus overcomes the estrangement of men from God and from one another and reveals to humankind a divinely liberated world in which truth and justice will increasingly prevail.

The task of theology, according to Cushman, is not so much intellectual as pastoral: it is, he writes, following Anselm, 'faith seeking understanding'.[9] Hence he looks to the shape of the liturgy, the sharing in worship and the sacraments as the way in which the faith is 'spoken' into being and brought to life.

The revival of interest in Wesleyan theology identified themes which resonated with the theology of the Boston personalism. However, together with process and liberation theologians Boston personalism tended to by-pass or ignore Christology and even dismiss it as nonsensical to modern man. How could one sensibly talk about 'incarnation'? Hence while they saw the importance of the teaching of Jesus, they focused worship on the personhood of the divine rather than the Trinity. Their emphasis was therefore on Jesus' humanity rather than his divinity and his moral example rather than his person. This limp interpretation of the person and work of Christ was challenged by Outler, Thomas Oden (b.1931) and Geoffrey Wainwright. Their study of Wesleyan theology encouraged them to restore the creeds to their central place in faith and worship and to recapture the spirit and confidence of the Early Church Fathers.

Serious attention to the person and work of Christ could not push on one side the question of his divine and human nature, nor could the worship of God avoid serious issues about his Trinitarian nature. On inspection an exclusive adherence to the

language of liberal theology was recognized to be without intellectual foundation. The exposition of the gospel had been dumbed
down to what was acceptable to the ordinary hearer and the conventional intellectual. The desire to feel at home in the modern
world, to follow the cultural fashion and to achieve evangelical
success had replaced the search for truth. The *zeitgeist* was
enthroned: sales growth was the key to reputation, church plant-
ing and membership numbers evidence of gospel-truth. But the
evidence disproved the thesis: a liberal theology did not mean
bums on seats. The time was ripe for a reconsideration of the
meaning of the Christian revelation.

Outler, Heizenrater, Cushman, Runyon and Wainwright found
in Wesleyan theology, a profound stimulus to attend to the tradition in the light of scripture, to affirm its reasonableness and
its correspondence with experience. All deny the inerrancy of
Scripture; all affirm the presence of God with his world. All believe
that God has in Christ committed himself to the perfecting of the
world; all proclaim that humankind has God-given freedom to
follow Christ, share in the world's perfecting and enjoy the soul's
desire for ultimate fulfilment. All believe that the world is open to
sensitive exploration; all believe that the Church has an essential
contribution to make to the well-being of human society; all
believe that all can be redeemed.

Christian faith is coherent and personally illuminating when it
is based on scripture, familiarity with the tradition, continuing
theological reflection and a determination to express itself in
worship and love of all creation.

III

The Experience of America: Theology Alive!

The openness of Methodist theology to enquiry and conversation
with the world is rooted in the expectation that we shall find God.
The purpose has been not only to grow in understanding of God,
but to bring together the world of human experience and offer it
to God in thanksgiving and worship. The bringing of the language

of scripture and tradition into relationship with the many disciplines, philosophies and styles of thinking open to humankind is
an aspect of missionary enterprise.

The American experience has given special vitality to Methodist
theology: it developed interactively with important philosophical
traditions. Rejection of any truck with predestinarianism, delivered theology into the liberty of personal enquiry, provided it
was based upon scripture and consistent with the tradition. Parker
Bowne (1847–1910) as we have seen was a major stimulus to open
creative theology since many found the Boston personalist school
particularly stimulating because it seemed to offer a language in
which the liveliness of God's creativity could be explored.

But it was not only personal idealism which stimulated theological enquiry. John Cobb (b. 1925) was intrigued by Whitehead's
philosophy of organism, later christened process philosophy.[10]
Whitehead had an interesting career. A Cambridge mathematician
who explored with Bertrand Russell the general conditions for
mathematical enquiry, he became Professor of Philosophy at
Harvard in 1924.[11] His interest in the most general conditions of
enquiry led him to focus on metaphysics. He calls the fundamental category of his system an actual occasion, which is not
something enduring but something in process of becoming. The
intention he announces in the preface to his magnum opus is 'to
construct a cosmological philosophy'.

> . . . it must be one of the motives of a complete cosmology,
> to construct a system of ideas which bring the aesthetic,
> moral, and religious interests into relation with those
> concepts of the world which have their origin in natural
> science.[12]

Taking up Whitehead's ideas, Cobb affirms that Christian theology holds together God and the world in a relationship which
recognizes both change, and movement towards an end. But he is
also aware that the dynamic of divine process must have preceded
the incarnation which leads him to develop a theology of the
eternal Logos which throws light on the doctrine of creation and
even the Wesleyan doctrine of perfection. He goes on to suggest

that while Christ is a way to God, he is not the only way: he takes, for example, a special interest in Theravada Buddhism. Interestingly Jacques Dupuis S. J. (1923–2004), a distinguished Roman Catholic theologian, argues for a position not wholly dissimilar.[13] Positive experience of Hinduism and Buddhism when he worked in India, led him to the conclusion that other ways of truth existed because they were permitted by God. Christian theology could learn from them. But if this was true, the assumption that knowledge of God was confined to the Church was questionable; it suggested the need to expand the christocentric model to embrace this insight. He adds that even this may be inadequate; we may need a more obviously theocentric model to do justice to the many visions and stories which sustain humanity's desire for God. God is present in his prevenient grace wherever we look with informed eyes. Bowne, Cobb and Dupuis all share the essential Methodist position of inclusivity. No statement of the Faith contains the whole truth; the conversation which God began with the world in creation will be enhanced by engaging with others who are on the same journey.

David Pailin (b.1936) is a welcome exception to the observation that UK Methodism has focused exclusively on historical and biblical studies and contributed little to theological thinking. On the other hand, he has had more influence in America than in the United Kingdom, which may say something about the interest British Methodism has in theological enquiry.[14] Pailin speaks of divine agency as a general teleological purpose and has worked consistently over many decades to develop his understanding of divine creativity in relation to the evolutionary processes. He holds together a self-giving God and creaturely choice in lively engagement within logical limits, in so doing illuminating both the nature of the divine and the qualities of creaturely choice.

Schubert Ogden (b.1928) also influenced by process theology, adopts a distinctive approach: he believes secularism provides the environment in which humankind finds God. The fact is that all human experience assumes a scientific world view but everyone has faith in God, even when they do not recognize it. The task of the theologian is to find words that will enable 'the believer' to name and give life to the faith that is within him, but this will be prompted not by rational discussion but by preaching. When God is named people 'see' that God is the ultimate ground of their sense of personal worth and the value of everything. God is Redeemer and Emancipator in the sense that as both immanent and other, he is able of his own free nature to fulfil the hope which is implicit in the freedom which human beings know themselves to enjoy. To learn to name and love God is to choose consciously to live the life of faith.

Carl Michalson (1915–1965), was a systematic theologian whose conversation was primarily with existentialist philosophy, particularly, Kierkegaard, Sartre and Merleau-Ponty. Scripture, theology, the life of Christ, the experience of worship and prayer were all judged from the point of their capacity to make a difference to human existence: their immediate historical impact was what was relevant and meaningful, not their historical facticity or their scientific justification. He affirmed the absolute individuality of each person, and their freedom to make their own way towards salvation independently of any presumed scientific understanding of the world. Nevertheless, he was persuaded of the immanence of God's grace and of his transforming power. Influenced in his approach to the New Testament by Rudolf Bultmann he, like Schubert Ogden, laid emphasis on the role of preaching. To be addressed by the gospel, could awaken a person now to an awareness of the presence of God in Christ and the freedom of life in him.

Stanley Hauerwas, a lay theologian, draws on a huge range of theological thinking from many traditions, yet his diverse experience is consistent with a continuing recognition that he stands within the world of Methodist theological enquiry. Less confident of the presence of God in the world, he believes that in order to proclaim the gospel to a world in need, the Christian Church must first be distinctive and accept responsibility to be the Kingdom of Grace. This is the community in which God dwells and which in its own life enjoys and celebrates the reality of God's presence. Worship is vital to this experience, especially the Eucharist.

James Cone (b.1938), a black American, was instrumental in taking Black theology in a new direction. He criticized the generalities of liberal theology because he argued that an understanding of God (a theology) must grow out of specific historical circumstances because God was incarnate in them. Black Americans therefore, had something to say about God which related to and grew out of their own experience of him. How was the experience of God mediated to them in the circumstances in which they found themselves?

Racial prejudice, poverty, lack of education and health care were all significant dimensions of their predicament. The freeing of the Israelites from oppression under Pharaoh, and the raising of Jesus were for them marks of God's work in history. By analogy, and without any consistent attempt to trace God's activity in the whole historical process, he identifies the bid of the Black community for freedom in America as another response of God to bring liberty to an oppressed community. He blames the white Church for its racism and willingness, intentionally as well as unconsciously, to oppress the poor and dispossessed. He drew not just on scripture, but on spirituals, jazz and the blues in order to give voice to the Black community.

The liberty which Christ offered has a political dimension which those who followed Christ cannot duck. This has implications for all Christians. Women's Liberation theology is one important consequence of the flourishing of Black theology, both of which have had considerable impact on the United Methodist Church and the Methodist Church of Great Britain. But God is working for the freedom of the oppressed whoever and wherever they are. Who the oppressed are is a serious matter for discernment in the light of faith: the oppressed, like the poor, are always with us.

IV

African and South American Contributions

Methodist conversation with God is not confined to twentieth-century Western philosophies. Kwesi Dickson (b.1929), a Ghanaian Methodist theologian has a special interest in the Old Testament. The way in which it holds together the natural world and tells and retells the historical experience of God's chosen people in the light of prophetic proclamation struck him as having much in common with traditional African religions. They provide a lively context in which the gospel comes to life, when one assumes that one is looking to name the God who is already present.

Mercy Oduyoye (b.1934), also a Ghanaian Methodist theologian, looks at African culture from a feminist perspective sympathetic to liberation theology. Her experience of theological debate in the WCC (she was Youth Secretary from 1967–1979, and Deputy General-Secretary from 1987–1994) confirmed her confidence in the Methodist vision. Methodism proclaims a gospel of freedom and grace which challenges oppressive attitudes towards women implicit in much African culture: it offers them the possibility of self-knowledge and hope which can liberate them to serve the world. In each case, African awareness of the spiritual provides good ground for recognizing the presence of God and telling the story of Jesus Christ and the freedom he brings.

José Miguez Bonino out of his experience of life in Argentina, found himself in conversation with revolutionary Marxism which he believed offered the most realistic account of the human condition in South America where society was deeply divided between the majority poor and an extremely wealthy minority.[15] Echoing the words of Marx, he wrote in 2006, 'Theology has to stop explaining the world and start transforming it'. His profound interest in liturgical celebration as the beginning of the possibility of change stemmed not just from a deep understanding of the Eucharist but also, by analogy, with South American dance which if entered into wholeheartedly launches change.[16]

He criticized Methodism for identifying itself too closely with the economic power of the capitalist West and its theological enquiry for withdrawing into the private world of the University. The Church should be actively working to change the world; theology should be the common possession of the people where its innate power to change people will bring hope. In many respects he recalls the world of John Wesley and proclaims a gospel closely related to his.

It is noteworthy that in none of these conversations is there evidence of a 'change of side'. Cobb is not a process philosopher; Bonino is not a Marxist; Michalson is not an existentialist; Kwesi Dickson does not 'revert' to traditional African religions; Oduyoye is not a liberation theologian; Cone is not a political activist. All of them, and many others to whom I could have drawn attention are, however, aware of the fact that there is much to learn, that human experience in its many forms and many formulations is God-given as is the intelligence and concern to study it, and that as a result it can provide encouragement, insight and new hope. And all this is because of their fundamental belief in the fact of God's prevenient grace and the expectation and hope arising from it that engagement with other philosophies and theologies will deepen their understanding of the Christian faith in general and the role of Methodist theology in particular. All are Methodists theologians.

V

Worship

Methodists understand that faith requires the nourishment and focus of worship. In worship Methodists gather up and offer to God in Christ all that they know, feel and believe. What we say in worship is not interior to the words of the service: they are informed and illuminated by the insights we take to them as a result of applying the language of scripture and tradition to the world of human enquiry. As we do so we share in the *missio dei*.

Wesley's theology was the product of bringing his understanding of scripture and tradition into relationship with his personal experience and the cultural environment in which he found himself. He was not hidebound by 'one' language of faith, he read and interpreted the many approaches of the Church Fathers; engaged with the philosophers of the Enlightenment, and was excited by the emerging results of scientific enquiry. He shared the Enlightenment perspective that all knowledge depended upon the senses though to regard him as a product of the Enlightenment is a mistake. The point is that he found the language of John Locke confirmed his view that humanity had no innate sense of God, and that the desire to seek God was God-given in the first instance through scripture and in experience. The question is still alive and worth exploring. The important point is that Wesley's reading of scripture and his wider reading of theology, led him to conclude, that given the God-given freedom which he affirmed every person to enjoy, no just and loving God would ever abandon humanity to its own devices. Hence the emphasis which he places on the doctrine of prevenient grace; God gives himself to his world in anticipation of humankind's becoming aware of him, or of the need for him.

Methodists take responsibility for themselves as a community when in the company of all the faithful, past, present and to come, they celebrate with thankfulness God's gracious redeeming presence. Naturally human beings feel out of place in assuming a relationship with God, but to keep our distance indicates a mistaken view of his nature. God is not censorious, or untrusting; he does not hold us to account for things beyond our power. To want God is already to begin to know his redeeming presence. As Augustine said, 'For who can call on Thee, not knowing Thee?'[17] God's courteous attention to his creation is manifest in Christ who assures us that everything necessary for our redemption has been accomplished; indeed it has been so from the beginning of creation and will be until the end of time. Trusting in Christ's revelation of the Father we lose all fear of God and are free to offer him in worship all that we are, all that we have and all that we hope for. We can focus all our attention on God and receive from him all that he is.

The recovery of Wesleyan theology has led us to see that this was Wesley's vision. Focused on the Trinity, Creator, Redeemer and Sustainer he was convinced that God's eternal presence with the world and with his people promises salvation for all who seek him. All are free to love God, to grow in understanding of him, to follow the way of Truth and offer true worship in spirit and in truth. At the heart of all worship is the Eucharist, the Lord's Supper, Holy Communion, when humankind celebrates with joy in word and deed the essential relationship of all creation with God, the Redemptive-Creator.

Methodist worship in the public mind is associated with preaching, hymn-singing and extempore prayer: all are important and continue to be so. It must never be forgotten, however, that Methodism was not only an evangelical revival, it was a sacramental renewal. Wesley refers to the means of grace as those 'outward signs, words, or actions, ordained by God, and appointed for this end, to be the ordinary channels whereby He might convey to men, preventing, justifying, or sanctifying grace.' . . . The chief of these means are prayer, whether in secret or with the great congregation; searching the Scriptures (which implies reading, hearing, and meditating thereon); and receiving the Lord's supper, eating bread and drinking wine in remembrance of him.[18]

The centrality of the Eucharist in early Methodism is underlined by Charles Wesley's publication of a special collection of hymns in 1745, *Hymns for the Lord's Supper* (1745). The Lord's Supper is celebrated as a sign and means of grace: a sense of real presence, if not the catholic understanding of the Real Presence lies behind the language, and I believe was actually in the mind of Charles when he wrote the lines.

Come, Holy Ghost, thine influence shed,
And realize the sign;
Thy life infuse into the bread,
Thy power into the wine.

Effectual let thy tokens prove,
And made by heavenly art,
Fit channels to convey thy love
To every faithful heart.[19]

The original context of Methodist worship was provided by the Book of Common Prayer. Wesley encouraged his followers to avail themselves of the worship of the parish church at least weekly on The Lord's Day in order to share in the Eucharist. This was honoured in the breech rather than in fact though many did so until they were excluded by the decision of bishops. In some parts of England, notably East Anglia, there remains until the present day a practice of occasional conformity which means that on certain feast days of the church calendar, Methodists worship with Anglicans in the local parish church and receive the elements of the bread and the wine if it is a Eucharist.

Wesley prepared an abbreviated version of the Book of Common Prayer, *the Sunday Service* which under Wesley's direction Richard Whatcoat and Dr Thomas Cook took with them to America in 1784. Wesley hoped that it would become the normal pattern of worship in America. And indeed, the 1784 Baltimore Conference which approved the formation of a Methodist Episcopal Church also agreed that the liturgy should be read at services and ministers, ordained according to the form prescribed by John Wesley, authorized to administer the sacraments. A British version followed in 1786.

Worship was a vital necessity consistently maintained; indeed, worship took place more than once on Sundays and often on other occasions during the week. But in practice, Methodists came to see little value in *reading* the liturgy, preferring freer forms of worship which spoke more directly to their condition and which were more comfortable for the itinerant minister, lay leader or circuit rider to conduct. They relied on the passion of extempore prayer, the immediacy of the preacher's response to the Word of God, the joyous singing of hymns and the impact of personal testimonies. Notwithstanding this, new liturgical books and helps for worship were issued independently in Britain, especially in Wesleyan Methodism over the next two centuries which show the continuing influence of forms of worship related to the *Book of Common Prayer*. The Primitive and United Methodist traditions published revised hymnbooks during the same period.

Significant events from the middle of the twentieth century brought about a major shift in Methodist worship which tended to resolve the uneasy tension between formal liturgy and free forms and encourage the recovery of a sacramental pattern.

First, there were the demands of the uniting Methodist churches in both Britain and America: they each needed a pattern of worship centrally developed and approved which would give the constituent members a sense of belonging and sharing a tradition. The major Methodist traditions in England, Primitive, United and Wesleyan came together in 1932; this led to the publication in 1936 of *The Book of Offices, being the Orders of Service authorized for Use in the Methodist Church together with the Order for Morning Prayer*. In 1939 the three major Methodist bodies in America, The Methodist Protestant Church, The Methodist Episcopal Church and The Methodist Episcopal Church South merged to form The Methodist Church. The result was the publication in 1945 of *The Book of Worship for Church and Home,* the first official worship book in American Methodism since *The Sunday Service,* which was retained for optional use.

Secondly, the rediscovery in the second half of the twentieth century of Wesley's theology and his firm devotion to the Eucharist — *The Lord's Supper* in much Methodist parlance — encouraged special attention to worship, above all to the sacraments of Baptism and Eucharist. The free form of worship with sermon was beginning to be thought inadequate as a full expression of the Church's thankfulness for the salvation wrought in Christ and for all God's mercies.[20]

The interest in liturgical forms was further stimulated, thirdly, by Pope John XXIII when he called the Second Vatican Council in 1959 in order, as he said, to open a window on the world. In so doing he lifted the eyes of all the Churches from mundane business to fundamental questions about the nature and practice of the Faith, and the relation of the Church and the world. The Council was constituted of some 2,300 fathers assisted by several thousand *periti* in theology, canon law and church history presided over by 12 cardinals. Observers represented the major churches not in communion with Rome. The impact was huge: never had there been such a gathering of priests, pastors, scholars focused on restating the Faith and re-structuring its practice for the contemporary world.

Significantly the first statement to be published on 4 December 1963 was the *Constitution on the Sacred Liturgy.* Its authorization of the vernacular for the celebration of the Eucharist stimulated ecumenical interest in the centrality of the liturgy in the life of the Church. Fourthly, with the abandonment of Latin as the official language of the Eucharist, the possibility existed to create an ecumenically agreed text for some elements of worship. If it could be achieved it would symbolize the community of worship among the churches, even if it fell far short of organic union. The Joint Liturgical Committee was established in 1963 consisting of all the major churches in Britain including the Roman Catholic. The purpose was wherever possible to agree texts for The Lord's Prayer, the creeds, lectionaries and forms for the celebration of the Eucharist. The parallel body in America was the Consultation on Common Texts which came into existence in the mid-60s.

Methodism was drawn into each of these movements. It was especially influenced by the revision of the Eucharist in Vatican II and played a full part in the resulting ecumenical discussions which led to new liturgies. They were not simply rewritings in contemporary language of the existing texts; rather they embodied the results of attention to the history of the liturgy, especially in regard to the sacraments of Baptism and Eucharist to make it possible for contemporary Christians to feel themselves part of the catholic tradition over time and space. The British Methodist Church produced *The Methodist Service Book* in 1975 and a further *Methodist Worship Book* in 1999. The United Methodist Church produced *The Book of Worship* in 1965. 'Supplemental Liturgical Resources' began to appear in 1971; these were included in a revised form in the *United Methodist Book of Worship* in 1992.

Throughout this period new hymn books were published in both America and Britain reflecting the continued importance of hymns in Methodist worship. In *Hymns and Psalms* (1983), the centrality of Charles and John Wesley hymns was confirmed: out of a total of 823 hymns 156 are by Charles Wesley and 16 by John.

The sacramental revival represents developments in worship which recover not only the Wesleyan perspective, but by recognizing Wesley's place in the catholic church, bring Methodist worship formally into the mainstream of Christian life – a position which many of us would say it had never left, though sometimes the forms and practices adopted by the Church did not express it. Charles Wesley's hymns appeared in the hymnbooks of many traditions because of the Eucharistic emphasis. In a striking doctoral thesis William Douglas Mills explores in parallel the current Eucharistic liturgies of Methodism and Roman Catholicism: their form and theology are very closely related.[21] There has also been a parallel development in Methodist ecclesiology though we lack as yet a major Methodist contribution to this aspect of theological enquiry. The most recent statement in British Methodism is significantly entitled, *Called to Love and Praise*.[22] The ongoing conversations between the World Methodist Council and the Roman Catholic Church and conversation between Methodism in Britain and the Roman Catholic Church have played a major role in reawakening their appreciation of John Wesley, his sacramental life and his ecclesiology.

Personal prayer figured prominently in the life of the ordinary Methodist. It was not self-centred, or inward-looking though it could be. In fact it involves affirming the presence of God in adoration, examination of conscience and confession, an honest asking for God's grace to meet personal demands in the context of an offering of the world's need in intercession. The whole begins and ends and is summed up in thankfulness.[23]

VI

A Faithful, Thankful Community in Love with God for the World's Sake

In each of these aspects of the Christian life, Methodists believe themselves to be responding to God's invitation in Christ to enter into conversation with him. Jesus encourages his disciples to join him in the conversation of prayer.

Our Father in heaven, hallowed be your name.
Your kingdom come.
Your will be done, on earth as it is in heaven.
Give us this day our daily bread.
And forgive us our debts,
As we also have forgiven our debtors.
And do not bring us to the time of trial,
But rescue us from evil.[24]

The attitude is present too in the Old Testament.[25]

In this conversation there is gathered up all our conversation within ourselves, with one another, with our world as we come more and more to love it and understand it. We offer it to God in full recognition of the fact of his continuing presence with his creation to perfect it.

It impacts upon the conversations within Methodism, in local societies, in districts and dioceses, in national and regional conferences, in the World Methodist Council, with our conversation with other traditions of the faith and with other Faiths. And perhaps (or perhaps it should!) especially in conversation with friends and neighbours.

The conversation is a praying, talking and learning so that we can take responsibility with God and with our fellow human beings for the well-being of one another, the creation and ourselves. In so doing we express our heartfelt thankfulness for God's commitment of himself to his world. This wholeness of feeling, believing is necessary in order to make a reality for ourselves and for our world of what we intuit to be the nature of creation. Methodists are *Called to Love and Praise*.

Author of life divine,
Who hast a table spread,
Furnished with mystic wine
And everlasting bread,
Preserve the life thyself hast given,
And feed and train us up for heaven.

Our needy souls sustain
With fresh supplies of love,
Till all thy life we gain,
And all thy fullness prove,
And strengthened by thy perfect grace,
Behold without a veil thy face.[26]

Conclusion

John Wesley met the needs of his generation with a compassion, courtesy and personal concern which stemmed from his deep awareness of God's gracious presence with him, with all people and with all creation. His theology, as has frequently been said, was practical. But practical theology is not to be distinguished from the serious task of making sense of what it means to talk about God. God is love-in-action. To know God's love is to want to understand him more; to want to understand him more is to want to trust him more so as to be freed to take the risk of loving the world in Christ's name for God's sake. Wesley was concerned to hold together in one seamless robe, the love of God and the love of the world and of all God's people.

Of course, his theological position was consistent with the orthodoxy of the generation in which he lived. Divine creation did not raise the same questions for him that it does for us: he did not have the advantage of the liberating work of Charles Darwin to take into account. Not having read Bultmann, he would have made no sense of demythologizing. Yet the liveliness of the Methodist conversation with God, in conference and through the work of scholars in their many societies – biblical scholarship, systematic theology, Christian ethics, pastoral theology, philosophical theology etc., points to the liberating inheritance with which Wesley endowed the Methodist people.

The result has been openness to human enquiry in the most general sense, an excitement with new knowledge, an awareness of new contexts for moral questioning, an unwillingness to settle for easy solutions and the recognition of just how much more there is to learn. Above all we have an appreciation of just how far we have fallen short of the glory of God – what it is to live out in our lives the love of God in Christ. We understand that however much is attempted, there is always more to do. But, as Wesley implied in his doctrine of perfection, it is always possible to do more, to understand more, to love more. And without love one will understand nothing.

The question for Methodists today is as it always has been, 'What is the gospel of Jesus Christ and how do we say it in our generation and in our location so as to introduce others (and in principle the world) into the excitement of lively conversation with God'? This is not a matter of 'doing good' – though there's nothing wrong with that – it is to recognize the divine call to involve the world in one conversation. Hence as God opens himself to show the inclusion of all creation in Christ, so we open ourselves to others and sit beside them, sharing bread and wine in celebration of God's presence with God's people. Without the increasing involvement of others, it is we not just they, who will be the poorer because without their contribution we shall be more ignorant and less affectionate than we could be. And it's not a case of what we *must* do to demonstrate our faith, it is a question of what we *can* do now that we are free and have quitted our fear. Far from being a burden, the pressures which flow from awareness of challenges to faith are the seeds of new understanding and as John Wesley said following St Paul, 'an enlargement of the heart'.[1]

John Wesley travelled far and wide to bear witness to God's forgiving presence. He ignored distance, tiredness and frustration: he recognized no boundaries because he rejected any thought that human institutions political, social, ecclesiological, economic could domesticate the love of God. But if boundaries do not exist, awareness of edges is crucial if one is to tackle new areas of enquiry as they emerge. Methodism affirms the presence of God and therefore approaches the contemporary challenges such as scientism, atheism, secularism, unbelief, war, climate change, world pollution, population growth, ignorance, political incompetence and economic greed – to mention but a few – without fear. After all God has preceded us: God's prevenient grace is present so there is no reason to be daunted. Methodism can freely look in every place and in every context, intellectual, moral, aesthetic and spiritual with hope and with the expectation of meeting God. We shall not work alone; we need the conversation of others if we are to make sense of it.

I referred in the first chapter to Kenneth Grayston's 1966 Inaugural Lecture in the University of Bristol where he referred to theology as exploration. He was absolutely right. Methodists might also agree with Mark C. Taylor when he writes:

> Religion is an emergent, complex, adaptive network of symbols, myths and rituals that, on the one hand, figure schemata of feeling, thinking and acting in ways that lend life meaning and purpose and, on the other, disrupt, dislocate and disfigure every stabilizing structure.[2]

But consider too Pistol, the loudmouthed associate of Falstaff in several of the plays of Shakespeare who has a fine line in bombastic language. When refused a loan by Falstaff on one occasion, he quips smartly:

> Why, then the world's mine oyster,
> Which I with sword will open.[3]

In like manner for Methodists the world is our oyster but we need no sword because the world has been opened already by God's grace so that we may find the pearl of great price. There is no dimension of our experience, whether opened up to us by science, technology, economics, historical enquiry, religious experience or aesthetics, that will fail to stimulate further understanding of what it is to believe in God, Father, Son and Holy Spirit and further ways of serving the world in Christ's name.

Methodists could take advantage of their freedom and within the framework of Christian orthodoxy, liturgical celebration and personal piety, move on with confidence to explore the exciting world of the twenty-first century. Perhaps they will: it will be interesting to see. Methodism is after all, a freedom movement, we are a pilgrim people, less attached to things and institutions, and more attached to God, his creation and his people.

We should sing the *Venite* more frequently and believe it!

Venite

Come, let us sing to the Lord
and rejoice in the rock, our Saviour.
Let us come and give thanks in his presence
and greet him with songs of praise.
The Lord is a great God,
a king supreme over all;
in his hands are the depths of the earth,
and the mountain heights are his;
the sea is his – he made it –
and the dry land was formed by his hands.
Come, let us kneel and adore,
let us worship the Lord our maker.
He is our God and we are his people,
the flock he leads with his hand.

Glory to the Father, and to the Son,
and to the Holy Spirit:
as it was in the beginning, is now,
and shall be for ever. Amen[4]

Notes

Preface

1   Kenneth Wilson, Joy in the Presence of the Crucified, in Paul M. Collins, Gerard Mannion, Gareth Powell and Kenneth Wilson (eds), *Christian Community Now*, 2008, London, T&T Clark, pp. 91–105.

Chapter 1

1   Kenneth Cracknell and Susan J. White, *An Introduction to World Methodism*, 2005, Cambridge, Cambridge University Press.
2   The Waldensians and the Methodist Church in Italy, while remaining independent churches, federated in 1979 and share one synod and one constitution.
3   Rupert E. Davies, *Methodism*, 1961, Harmonsworth, Penguin Books, second revised edition, London, Epworth Press, 1976. Chapter 1 *passim*.
4   See, for example, James Dunn, 1990, *Unity and Diversity in the New Testament*, London, SCM Press; Charles Freeman, 2009, *A New History of Early Christianity*, London and New Haven, Yale University Press.
5   W. R. Ward, 1992, *The Protestant Evangelical Awakening*, Cambridge, Cambridge University Press.
6   St. Francis de Sales, 1950, *Introduction to the Devout Life*, trans. John K. Ryan, New York, Harper and Row.
7   I think it could be argued that it is an analogous excess and moral confusion today that has provoked a renewed conservatism in Roman Catholicism, John Milbank's radical orthodoxy and Stanley Hauerwas's emphasis on the Church as the community of grace.
8   See: John Kent, *Wesley and the Wesleyans*, 2002, Cambridge, Cambridge University Press; J. C. D. Clark, The Eighteenth Century Context, in William J. Abraham and James E. Kirby (eds), 2009, *The Oxford Handbook of Methodist Studies*, Oxford, Oxford University Press, pp. 13–19.
9   The term 'Enlightenment' emerged only in the nineteenth century to cover philosophical developments of this period.
10 The novelist, Maryanne Robinson, discusses the general point in her intriguing book, *Absent Mind*, 2010, New Haven, Yale.
11 John Brewer, *The Pleasures of the Imagination: English Culture in the Eighteenth Century*, 1997, London, HarperCollins, pp. 98–122.

Notes

12 Angela Shier-Jones, Conferring as Theological Method, in Clive Marsh, Brian Beck, Angela Shier Jones and Helen Waring (eds), 2004, *Methodist Theology Today: Unmasking Methodist Theology,* New York, Continuum, pp. 82–94.

13 'Homo sum; humani nil a me alienum puto'. – 'I am a man, I count nothing human indifferent to me.' Terence, *Heautontimorumenos,* 1. i. 25.

14 Simone Weil, Attention and Will, *Gravity and Grace,* 1952, London, Routledge and Kegan Paul, pp. 105–11. See also, Iain McGilchrist, 2009, *The Master and His Emissary: The Divided Brain and the Making of the Western World,* New Haven and London, Yale University Press, pp. 28–9.

15 *Holy Communion,* The Methodist Worship Book, 1999, Peterborough, England, Methodist Publishing House, p. 197.

16 Kenneth Grayston, 1966, London, Epworth Press.

17 Rom. 8. 18.

18 John Wesley, *Sermons on Several Occasions,* Vol. 1, written in 1745, published in 1746.

Chapter 2

1 Albert C. Outler, The Wesleyan Quadrilateral, in Thomas A. Langford (ed.), 1991, *Doctrine and Theology in The United Methodist Church,* Nashville, TN: Abingdon Press, pp. 75–88.

2 Changes in our approach to the Bible came in the nineteenth century. Methodism produced many outstanding Biblical Scholars whose work has rescued Methodist theology from the taint of fundamentalism. Apart from Wesley Studies it is, with notable exceptions, the only field in which British Methodism has a distinguished scholarly record. See below Chapter 7.

3 See below Chapter 9.

4 John Henry Newman, *An Essay in the Development of Doctrine,* 1845, 1989, sixth edition, South Bend, Notre Dame University Press, quoted in John Cornwell, *Newman's Unquiet Grave,* 2010, London, Continuum, p. 88.

5 Wesley, Works of John Wesley, 1975 – , Nashville, Abingdon, Vol. i. 105–6; quoted in Gennifer Benjamin Brooks, Preaching, in *The Oxford Handbook of Methodist Studies,* Oxford, Oxford University Press, 2009, pp. 369–70.

6 Timothy Fuller (ed.), 1989, *The Voice of Liberal Learning: Michael Oakeshott on Education,* New Haven and London, Yale University Press.

7 See Conference Resolution on 'The Doctrinal Standards of the Methodist Church', *Minutes of the British Methodist Conference,* 2010, Peterborough, UK Methodist Publishing, p. 28.

8 See below Chapter 6.

9 It is a moot point whether this should be called the first Anglican or the first Methodist hymnbook, since at that time the Wesleys were involved in working with the Anglican Church in America having responded to an appeal by the Bishop of London.

Notes

10 *A Collection of Hymns for the Use of the People called Methodists,* The Works of John Wesley, Vol. 7, ed. Franz Hildebrandt and Oliver A. Beckerlegge, Oxford, Clarendon Press, 1983, Preface, p. 74.

11 Ibid.

12 J. Ernest Rattenbury, *The Eucharistic Hymns of John and Charles Wesley,* 1948, London, Epworth Press.

13 *A Collection of Hymns for the Use of the People called Methodists* op. cit. No. 2.

14 Ibid. No. 29.

15 Ibid. No. 114.

16 Ibid. No. 241.

17 Ibid. No. 364.

18 Ibid. No. 505.

Chapter 3

1 Donald A. Schon, *The Reflective Practitioner,* London, Temple Smith, 1983.

2 See de Caussade, *Abandonment to Divine Providence,* 1921, Exeter, Catholic Records Office. De Caussade is marvelously encouraging in this regard. If Our Lord has commanded his disciples to be perfect as their Father in heaven is perfect, it must be possible: the point is to understand sensitively what perfection means and not to beat oneself to death every time we fail! Cf. Wesley's much misunderstood but very helpful doctrine of perfection to which, in my opinion, we would do well to give more thought.

3 John Wesley, Sermon XXX and XXXI, *Forty Four Sermons,* 1944, London, Epworth Press.

4 Ibid. pp. 411–12.

5 This does not mean that Wesley should be thought of as a 'Liberation Theologian', but it does suggest that he would have had no difficulty in understanding the slogan 'option of preference for the poor'.

6 Randy L. Maddox, *Responsible Grace,* 1994, Nashville, TN, Abingdon Press.

7 By 1760 there were more than thirty circuits (twenty in England, seven in Ireland and two each in Scotland and Wales), and one hundred itinerant preachers. See below, Chapter 9, for discussion of the organization and management of the Methodist Movement as 'a faithful family'.

8 John Wesley, *Primitive Physic: An Easy and Natural Method of Curing Most Diseases* (first published anonymously 1747, published with acknowledged authorship 1760), Nashville, TN, United Methodist Publishing House, 1992. Preface.

9 Wesley attacks Rousseau in para. 19 of his sermon on *The Unity of the Divine Being* (No. 114 in Thomas Jackson edition, 1872) because he lays all his emphasis on duty to neighbour, neglecting the associated duty to God. Nevertheless, his sympathy with the condition of a natural state attributed

to the Indian, shares some common features with Rousseau. Cf. Jean-Jacques Rousseau, *Discourse on the Origin and Foundation of Inequality Among Mankind*, 1755, *The Social Contract or Principles of Political Right*,1762.

10 Ibid.

11 Ibid.

12 Interestingly Newman ran into analogous criticism when appointed tutor at Oriel College in 1822.

13 A scanned version of the 1821 edition of *A Christian Library* in 30 volumes is available online at Wesley Centre for Applied Theology.

14 Kingswood School removed to Bath in 1851.

15 *A Short Account of the School in Kingswood, near Bristol.* First published in 1749: reprinted in facsimile in 1963.

16 A. G. Ives, *Kingswood School in Wesley's Day and Since,* 1970, London, Epworth Press, p. 46 (14l is £14.00, a not inconsiderable sum in the circumstances of the time).

17 Ibid. p. 48.

18 Michael Oakeshott, Education: The Engagement and Its Frustration, in Timothy Fuller (ed.), *The Voice of Liberal Learning: Michael Oakeshott on Education*, 1989, New Haven and London, Yale University Press, p. 63.

19 Ibid.

20 *Hymns and Psalms*, 1983, London, Methodist Publishing House, No. 795. *Hymns and Psalms,* the current hymn book of the British Methodist Church, is described on the title page as *A Methodist and Ecumenical Hymn Book.* The British Conference of 1979 invited other denominations to share in putting it together which indicates how British Methodism was thinking about its role within the Church Catholic at the time. In fact, the Baptist Union, Churches of Christ, Church of England, Congregational Federation, Methodist Church in Ireland, United Reform Church and the Wesleyan Reform Union accepted the invitation.

21 *A Collection of Hymns for the Use of the People Called Methodists*, op.cit. No. 311.

22 Judith A. Merkle offers stimulating reflection on these themes in *Being Faithful*, 2010, London and New York, T&T Clark. The fact that the book is written from a Catholic perspective is informative of the growing relationship between 'servant theology' in Methodism and Roman Catholicism.

Chapter 4

1 Paul Tillich, *Systematic Theology,* Vol. 1, 1953, London, James Nisbet, p. 3.

2 Thomas A. Langford, *Practical Divinity: Theology in the Wesleyan Tradition*, 1983, Nashville, TN, Abingdon Press, p. 24.

3 The Roman Catholic Church affirms that no one is predestined to hell. *Catechism of The Catholic Church*, 1994, London, Geoffrey Chapman, para. 1037.

Notes

4   John Wesley, The Question, 'What is an Arminian?' Answered by a Lover of Free Grace (third edition, 1872), *The Works of John Wesley*, Thomas Jackson (ed.), Rpt. Grand Rapids, MI, 1978, Vol. 10, p. 358.

5   See, for example, John Wesley, *Predestination Calmly Considered*, 1752.

6   Ibid. VI quoting *The Westminster Confession*, Chapter 3.

7   Ibid. XLII. 'Our Blessed Lord does indisputably command and invite "all men everywhere to repent" [Acts 17:30]. He sends his ambassadors, in his name, "to preach the gospel to every creature" [Mk. 16:15]. He himself "preached deliverance to the captives" [Lk. 4:8]. XLIII. It is not written, "God is justice," or "God is truth" (although he is just and true in all his ways). But it is written, "God is love" [1 Jn. 4:8] (love in the abstract, without bounds), and "there is no end to his goodness" [cf. Ps. 52:1]. His love extends even to those who neither love nor fear him. He is good, even to the evil and unthankful; yes, without any exception or limitation, to all the children of men. For "the Lord is loving" (or good) "unto every man, and his mercy is over all his works"' [Ps, 145:9, B.C.P.].

8   Cf. Ivor H. Jones and Kenneth B. Wilson (eds), *Freedom and Grace,* 1988, London, Epworth Press.

9   Richard Watson, *Theological Institutes,* 1843, New York, G. Lane and P. P. Sandford.

10 See below, Chapter 5.

11 Sermon 55 in Thomas Jackson, Works of John Wesley, 1872.

12 Charles Wesley, *Hymns on the Trinity,* 1767, No. 109; Franz Hildebrandt and Oliver Beckerlegge, The Works of John Wesley, Vol. 7, *A Collection of Hymns for the Use of the People called Methodists,* Oxford, Clarendon Press, 1983, No. 251; *Hymns and Psalms,* No. 6, omitting verse 5.

13 Frank Whaling (ed.), 'Introduction', in *John and Charles Wesley: Selected Prayers, Hymns and Journal Notes, Sermons, Lectures and Treatises,* 1981, Mahway, NJ: Paulist Press, p. 8. Quoted in Seng-Kong Tan, The Doctrine of the Trinity in John Wesley's Prose and Poetic Works, *Journal for Christian Theological Research* 7, 2002, p. 3.

14 John Miley, *Systematic Theology,* 1892; Thomas Summer, *Systematic Theology,* 1888.

15 Geoffrey Wainwright, *Doxology,* 1980, London, Epworth Press; New York, Oxford University Press.

16 Raymond E. Brown, *The Gospel According to John,* 1966, London, Geoffrey Chapman, p. 617.

17 These words are Raymond E. Brown's translation.

18 Jn. 14. 8–13.

19 Matt. 6. Gal. 4. vv. 4–7.

20 Gal. 4. vv. 4–7.

21 The Works of John Wesley, Vol. 5, *A Collection of Hymns for the Use of the People Called Methodists,* ed. Franz Hildebrandt and Oliver A. Beckerlegge, 1983, Oxford, Clarendon Press, No. 225.

22 Op. cit. No. 242. The section is entitled, '*For Believers Rejoicing*'.

23 Rom. 8: 14–17.

24 St Augustine, *Confessions,* 1907, trans. E. B. Pusey, London, Dent, Everyman's Library, Bk1, ch. 1.
25 An example from a recent writer on spirituality makes my point, 'Growing into God is not so much, then, a process of becoming perfect. Perfection is a human ideal, an arrogant one at that, but it is not a human state. Perfection is not ours to have. On the contrary, to aspire to perfection is to doom ourselves to the kind of failure that can lead either to depression or despair – neither of which is healthy, both of which only distract from the real purpose of life.' *For All that has been, Thanks*, Rowan Williams and Joan Chichester OSB, 2010, Norwich, Canterbury Press, p. 96.
26 Thomas A. Langford does not even allude to it in his *Practical Divinity – Theology in the Wesleyan Tradition*, 1983, Nashville, TN, Abingdon.
27 William J. Abraham, Christian Perfection, in *The Oxford Handbook of Methodist Studies*, 2009, Oxford, Oxford University Press, p. 587.
28 Albert C. Outler (ed.), *John Wesley*, 1964, New York, Oxford University Press.
29 Matt. 5, 48.
30 J. P. de Caussade, *Abandonment to Divine Providence,* trans. E. J. Strickland, 1921, Exeter, Catholic Records Press. Wesley will not have been familiar with this work of de Caussade since it was not published in French until 1867, but he was certainly familiar with the Catholic tradition of ascetic theology in which de Caussade stands.

Chapter 5

1 St Thomas Aquinas, *Summa Theologiae,* 1a–2ae, cix.6.
2 Karl Rahner, Nature and Grace, *Theological Investigations,* Vol. IV. Quoted in Gerald A. McCool, *A Rahner Reader,* 1975, London, Darton, Longman and Todd, p. 183.
3 John Wesley, Sermons, Thomas Jackson (ed.), 1972, No. 85 on the text, Phillipians 2: 12–13.
4 Karl Rahner, Nature and Grace, in *Theological Investigations*, Vol. IV, 1966, London, Darton, Longman and Todd; Baltimore, MD, Helicon Press, p. 183.
5 Thomas A. Langford, *Practical Divinity – Theology in the Wesleyan Tradition,* 1983, Nashville, TN, Abingdon Press, p. 27.
6 Karl Rahner, op.cit. p. 180.
7 Karl Rahner, op.cit. p. 180.
8 Asa Shinn, *An Essay on the Plan of Salvation*, 1813.
9 John Wesley: Sermon IX, *The Spirit of Bondage and of Adoption,* para. 6.
10 Paul Tillich, *Systematic Theology,* Vol. 3, 1964, London, James Nisbet, pp. 239–43.
11 For some reason the words are omitted in the otherwise excellent Easter Vigil in *The Methodist Book of Worship,* 1999, Peterborough, Methodist Publishing House, pp. 265–80.

Notes

12 Stanley Hauerwas, Salvation even in Sin: Learning to Speak Truthfully about Ourselves, *Sanctify Them in the Truth,* 1998, ed. Iain Torrance and Bryan Spinks, Edinburgh, T&T Clark, p. 73.

13 St. Irenaeus, *Adversus Haereses,* IV, 20, 7. We know that John Wesley was familiar with the writings of St. Irenaeus. He refers to him, for example, in *Plain Account of Genuine Christianity,* 1753, section 11.

14 Rom. 3:21–6.

15 Adopted at Baltimore Conference of 1784. See *United Methodist Church Book of Discipline,* 2008, para. 103.

16 *Deed of Union,* 1932, section 2, para. 4.2, Purposes and Doctrines.

17 John Wesley, *The Doctrine of Original Sin, According to Scripture, Reason, and Experience,* Bristol, 1757.

18 Gen. 1:26–7.

19 John Wesley, *Forty-four Sermons,* London, Epworth Press, Sermon V, pp. 49–60.

20 Wilbur Fisk Tillett, *Personal Salvation,* 1902, Nashville, TN, Methodist Publishing House, South.

21 Cf. for example Richard Wilkinson and Kate Pickett, *The Spirit Level,* 2009, London, Allen Lane. Both writers are, interestingly, health economists not politicians. The statistical analysis has been questioned but the general position is widely accepted to be a potential ingredient of national and international cohesion.

22 The substance of this formed the 27th Fernley Hartley Lecture delivered at the Wesleyan Conference in 1897; London, Charles H. Kelly, 1898. Edinburgh, 1902, T&T Clark.

23 Edinburgh, 1902, T&T Clark.

24 *Spiritual Principle of the Atonement* (pp. 226–7), and *The Fatherhood of God,* p. 288.

25 Thomas A. Langford (ed.), John Wesley and Theological Method in Randy Maddox, *Rethinking Wesley's Theology for Contemporary Methodism,* 1998, Nashville, TN, Abingdon, Kingswood Books, p. 35.

Chapter 6

1 John Wesley, *The New Creation,* Sermon 64, Thomas Jackson edition, 1872.

2 *Ad Gentes,* para. 1.

3 Ibid. para. 2.

4 See *The Catechism of the Catholic Church,* 1994, London, Geoffrey Chapman, paras. 849–56.

5 *Called to Love and Praise,* 1999, Peterborough, Methodist Publishing House, 2.1.2. and 2.1.4.

6 Ibid. 3.2.1.

7 The statement has authority because it is now included in the United Methodist Church *Book of Discipline,* the Church's official law book.

8   Matt. 28: 5b–10; 16–20.

9   *Hymns and Psalms*, London, Methodist Publishing House, 1983, No. 811, v. 2.

10 *A Collection of Hymns for the Use of the People called Methodists*, 1983, Oxford, Clarendon Press, No. 271, v. 2.

11 Ibid. No. 305, v. 2.

12 Ibid. No. 464, vv. 1–2. Interestingly this comes from a section called, 'For Believers Interceding for the World.'

13 See below, Chapter 7.

14 *John Wesley,* Albert C. Outler, 1964, New York, Oxford University Press, pp. 493–9.

15 Ibid. pp. 493–4.

16 Distinguished alumni include George Bernard Shaw (Nobel Prize for Literature) and Ernest Walton, physicist, who later became also a pupil of Methodist College, Belfast, who is the only Irish winner of a Nobel Prize for science.

17 Boards on the walls of the offices of the British Methodist Church record the names. The offices were formerly those of the Methodist Missionary Society.

18 Thomas Coke, 1783, *A Plan of the Society for the Establishment of Missions amongst the Heathens.*

Chapter 7

1   *Called to Love and Praise*, statement on ecclesiology adopted in 1999 by British Methodist Conference.

2   Cf. Rom. 12.2. Do not be conformed to this world, but be transformed by the renewing of your minds, so that you may discern what is the will of God – what is good and acceptable and perfect.

3   A superb discussion of Wesley's position, especially in relation to Aquinas' thinking, is to be found in D. Stephen Long, *John Wesley's Moral Theology*, 2005, Nashville, TN, Abingdon Press.

4   Mary Warnock argues that religion should be kept out of politics. In the sense that she discusses it she is right. There is no substitute for sound moral argument: religious faith offers no privileged access to God for solutions on moral questions. However, this does not mean that theological enquiry is irrelevant, concerned as it is with what it is to be human and how to enable that to flourish. Reflection on the story which Christianity tells, with its illuminating speculation on what counts as truly personal behaviour can contribute to sound judgement. Cf. Mary Warnock, *Dishonest to God*, 2010, London, Continuum.

5   Jn. 1. 1–5. For shrewd and rewarding discussion see C. K. Barrett, *The Gospel According to St John*, 1955, London, SPCK. This commentary, dated as it is

Notes

in some respects, is still a major achievement by the doyen of Methodist New Testament scholars.

6   Gingrich and Arndt, *A Greek-English Lexicon of the New Testament,* 1957, Chicago, IL, Chicago University Press, s.v.

7   Rom. 8. 22.

8   Phil. 2. 12c.

9   David Hempton, *Methodism,* 2005, New Haven, Yale University Press, p. 179 and chapter 8 in general, 'Consolidation and Decline'.

10 Stanley Hauerwas, *A Community of Character,* 1981, Notre Dame, Notre Dame University Press; *Wilderness Wanderings,* 1997, Boulder, CO, Westview Press.

11 Stanley Hauerwas, *Hannah's Child – A Theological Memoir,* 2010, London, SCM Press, p. 231.

12 Philip Jenkins, *Jesus Wars,* 2010, London, SPCK, tells the colourful story of the Church's pursuit of the truth about Jesus – human or divine?

13 Matt.22.37. Cf. Deut. 6.5. It is interesting that the Hebrew word translated 'might' in Deut. 6.5. is rendered by the author of Matthew's Gospel with the Greek word *dianoia* which means 'intellect'.

14 Phil. 2.5. No reputable commentator currently denies that St Paul is the author of this epistle.

15 Daniel D. Whedon, *Essays, Reviews and Discourses,* 1887, New York, Phillips and Hunt, p. 110.

16 I would have said 'Dogma' but its meaning has been lost: the term in the public mind means, 'prejudiced', 'unthinking' and even 'irrelevant'. In fact it is a neutral term meaning, 'settled opinion' or 'a doctrine laid down with authority'.

17 *Practical Divinity,* 1983, is the title of Thomas Langford's volume on Theology in the Wesleyan Tradition, Nashville, Abingdon Press; *Reasonable Faith,* 2010, London, Routledge, is a collection of essays by John Haldane, an exposition of Catholic philosophical themes, Thomistic in character.

18 *Hymns and Psalms,* 1983, London, Methodist Publishing House, No. 404.

19 J. L. Mackie, *The Miracle of Theism,* 1982, Oxford, Oxford University Press, chapter 9, The Problem of Evil, pp. 150–76.

20 Ed. Williams J. Abraham and James E. Kirby, 2009, Oxford, Oxford University Press.

21 Carl Michalson, *Worldly Theology,* 1967, New York, Charles Scribner's Sons.

22 C. A. Coulson, *Science and Christian Faith,* 1955, Oxford, Oxford University Press, second edition, 1971, London, Collins. Charles Coulson was a distinguished scholar in mathematics, physics, chemistry and molecular biology. He was successively Rowse Ball Professor of Applied Mathematics and the first Professor of Theoretical Chemistry in the University of Oxford. The chair in Theoretical Chemistry is now named after him.

23 Herbert Butterfield, *The Origins of Modern Science,* 1949, London, Bell & Sons.

24 Bernard Lonergan S. J., *Insight,* 1992, fifth edition, Toronto, University of Toronto Press.

Notes

Chapter 8

1   J. L. Austin, *How to do Things with Words*, 1962, ed. J. O. Urmson, Oxford, Oxford University Press.
2   Jer. 18.1–4.
3   Gen. 1.3, 6, 9, 11, etc; Matt. 17. 5b ; Lk. 9. 35.
4   Deut. 6.4–7.
5   Deut. 8.11.
6   Deut. 8.18–19.
7   Deut. 16.15.
8   Rom. 8.31, 38.
9   Thomas A. Langford, *Practical Divinity – Theology in the Wesleyan Tradition*, 1983, Nashville, TN, Abingdon Press, p. 21.
10 In my view we should be careful not to use the word 'literal'; the term is too restricted in capturing Wesley's more judicious approach.
11 Sarah Heaner Lancaster, Scripture and Revelation, in William J. Abraham and James E. Kirby (eds), 2009, *The Oxford Handbook of Methodist Studies*, Oxford, Oxford University Press, p. 489.
12 Ian Paisley was a founder and minister of The Free Presbyterian Church, established in the face of what he regarded as the fall from grace of the Presbyterian Church. He became the First Minister of Northern Ireland in 2007.
13 Leslie Weatherhead, *The Christian Agnostic*, 1965, London, Lutterworth, p. 124.
14 Ibid. p. 120.
15 Ibid. p. 123.
16 Ibid. p. 163.
17 The Revised Version is known in the United States as American Standard Version, 1901.
18 World Council of Churches, Faith and Order Commission Paper No. 111, Geneva, 1982.
19 Methodism's ecumenical involvement is underlined in Geoffrey Wainwright, *Methodists in Dialogue,* 1995, Nashville, TN, Abingdon Press.
20 Geoffrey Wainwright, *Methodists in Dialog,* 1995, Nashville, TN, Kingswood Books, Abingdon Press, p. 9.

Chapter 9

1   A. J. Ayer, *Language, Truth and Logic,* 1936, London, Gollancz.
2   Thomas J. Altizer and Robert Hamilton, *Radical Theology and the Death of God*, 1966, New York, Bobbs-Merrill; Thomas J. Altizer, *The Gospel of Christian Atheism*, 1966, Philadelphia, PA, Westminster Press.
3   Rupert E. Davies, John Newton, Raymond George, John Kent and John Vickers are some of those who made significant contributions to the study of Methodist history.

Notes

4 Re-published on CD-ROM, 1994, Franklin, TN, Providence House.

5 The Bicentennial Edition of the Works of John Wesley, 1975 –, Oxford, Oxford University Press; 1984 – , Nashville, TN, Abingdon Press.

6 Albert C. Outler, *John Wesley*, 1964, New York, Oxford University Press.

7 Theodore Runyon, *The New Creation: John Wesley's Theology Today*, UME Press.

8 Theodore Runyon (ed.), *Sanctification and Liberation: Liberation Theologies in the Light of the Wesleyan Tradition*, 1981, Nashville, TN, Abingdon.

9 Robert E. Cushman, *Faith Seeking Understanding*, 1981, Durham, NC, Duke University Press.

10 Alfred North Whitehead, *Process and Reality: An Essay in Cosmology*, 1929, New York, Macmillan; reprinted 1959, New York, Harper and Brothers.

11 Russell and Whitehead, *Principia Mathematica* 1910–1913, 3 vols, Cambridge, MA, Cambridge University Press.

12 Ibid. p. vi.

13 Jacques Dupuis S. J., *Towards a Christian Theology of Religious Pluralism*, 1998, Maryknoll, NY, Orbis Books.

14 David Pailin, *God and the Processes of Reality: Foundations for a Credible Theism*, 1989, London, Routledge. Darren J. N. Middleton, *David Pailin's Theology of Divine Action*, Process Studies, Vol. 22, No. 4, Winter 1993, pp. 215–26.

15 Jose Miguez Bonino, *Doing Theology in a Revolutionary Situation*, 1979, Philadelphia, PA, Fortress Press.

16 A view he shared with Tissa Balasuriya, O. M. I., *Eucharist and Human Liberation*, 1979, Maryknoll, Orbis Books. To share in the Eucharist was to share in the dynamic of God's liberation of all humanity through Christ: peace, justice and reconciliation.

17 St. Augustine, *Confessions*, trans. E. B. Pusey, 1907, London, Dent, Everyman's Library, Bk.1, ch.1, p. 1.

18 John Wesley, *Forty-Four Sermons*, 1944, London, Epworth Press, Sermon XII, The Means of Grace, p. 136.

19 Charles Wesley, *Hymns for the Lord's Supper*, 1745; Hymns and Psalms, 1983, London, Methodist Publishing House, No. 602.

20 Newman when he was Vicar of St Mary's, the University Church in Oxford, was renowned as a great preacher. But he was clear, as a recent biographer says that preaching was not everything that was required in worship. '. . . preaching cannot be an end in itself, he counseled; it is a prelude to the Church's salvation – a theme that he would develop, expand, and take in new directions, in the next stage of his Oxford ministry. Preaching, he insisted, is no substitute for the sacraments – means and pledges of grace, – keys which open the treasure – house of mercy'. John Cornwell, *Newman's Unquiet Grave*, 2010, London, Continuum, p. 51.

21 William Douglas Mills, '"*We are the Church*" *The Romanisation of United Methodism 1945–1988*', Unpublished thesis, 2002, Texas Tech. University.

22 The Methodist Conference of 1999 gave it official status when it was agreed to be a Conference Statement.

23 The best discussion of prayer by a Methodist – and especially for any person, Christian or not, who wants to pray and not merely to learn about

praying – is undoubtedly, J. Neville Ward, *The Use of Praying*, 1967, London, Epworth Press.

24 Matt. 6.9–13.

25 'Come now, let us argue it out, says the Lord: though your sins are like scarlet, they shall be like snow; though they are red like crimson, they shall become like wool.' The AV has, 'Come now, let us *reason* together. . . .' (Is. 1.18).

26 Charles Wesley, *Hymns for the Lord's Supper*, 1745; *Hymns and Psalms*, 1983, London, Methodist Publishing House, No. 596.

Conclusion

1 2 Corinthians 6:11.

2 Mark C. Taylor, *After God*, 2007, London and New Haven, Yale University Press. Quoted in review by Simon Blackburn, Times Higher Education Supplement, 23 November 2007, p. 21.

3 William Shakespeare, *The Merry Wives of Windsor*, Act II, Sc. ii, l.1.

4 Psalm 95, vv. 1–7. Prayer in the Morning, *Methodist Worship*, Peterborough, UK, Methodist Publishing House, 1999, p. 6.

Index

Index

Index

Index